BERNARD SHAW

a pictorial biography

BY MARGARET SHENFIELD

THAMES AND HUDSON · LONDON

To my mother and father

Note
Most of the quotations which are not identified in the text are taken from Shaw's *Sixteen Self-Sketches*, his correspondence with Ellen Terry, the prefaces to his plays, and Beatrice Webb's *Our Partnership*.

© *Margaret Shenfield 1962*
Printed in Great Britain by
Jarrold & Sons Ltd Norwich

Killiney Bay, where Shaw had his first swimming-lesson

GEORGE BERNARD SHAW was born at 33 Synge Street, Dublin, on 26 July 1856, 'the fruit of an unsuitable marriage between two quite amiable people who finally separated in the friendliest fashion and saw no more of one another after spending years together in the same house without sharing one another's tastes, activities or interests. They and their children never quarrelled: though not an emotional household it was not an unkindly one.'

His mother had received the genteel education considered suitable for the daughter of a 'country gentleman', so that at the time of her marriage she had no marketable skills, no knowledge of how to house-keep without a staff of servants, and very little experience of the ways of the world. She married George Carr Shaw, a man some twenty years older than herself, with a squint, a pension of £60 a year, a mill whose steady decline he was totally unable to prevent, and a sense of comic anticlimax which Shaw remembered and quoted at intervals throughout his life.

Unfortunately it was not until after the wedding that Mrs Shaw discovered in her husband a fault which she had not suspected in the least and which was

33 Synge Street, Dublin;
Shaw's birthplace

to accelerate the downfall of the family's fortunes: George Carr Shaw was a chronic drunkard, who, without the slightest intention of doing any harm, speedily shifted all his household and other responsibilities on to her shoulders. Not that he was a difficult man to live with: the greatest disasters left him unruffled. When, for instance, his firm went bankrupt, the other partner gave way to tears; Shaw merely retired to a quiet corner and burst into peals of laughter at the ludicrous solemnity of the affair. But this lack of temperament was only a passive virtue where practical living was concerned. His most positive contribution to the formation of his son's character was the mockery of solemnity he instilled into him.

'When I was a child he gave me my first dip in the sea in Killiney Bay. He prefaced it by a very serious exhortation on the importance of learning to swim, culminating in these words: "When I was a boy of only fourteen my knowledge of swimming enabled me to save your Uncle Robert's life." Then, seeing I was deeply impressed, he stooped, and added confidentially in my ear, "and, to tell you the truth, I never was so sorry for anything in my life afterwards."'

Shaw's father (extreme right),
his mother (extreme left),
and George Vandaleur Lee
(seated, centre), who taught Mrs Shaw
singing and formed Bernard's
musical taste when he was a boy

Mr Shaw was very unlike the Napoleons, Stalins, and Mussolinis whom his son came to admire. On the other hand, his wife had something of their single-mindedness. Burdened with a drunken husband, an income which rarely much exceeded £100 a year, three children, and an obligation (as she felt) to keep up an appearance of respectability and put a barrier between her family and the tradesmen or working-class neighbours who were probably better off than they, she never weakened and never lost her temper. She was an impassive woman, not given to emotion, even the maternal emotion. Her children, and the housekeeping generally, were left mainly in the hands of servants, who formed their characters by threatening that a cock would come down the chimney if they were naughty, and provided for their entertainment by taking them with them on visits to relatives in the slums of Dublin, which thoroughly disgusted Shaw.

Mrs Shaw had only one absorbing interest: she was passionately devoted to singing, which she studied under George Vandaleur Lee, a Dublin teacher and conductor who had perfected an unusually harmless method of voice-training in

George Vandaleur Lee

an age when girls were often forced into florid coloratura, in emulation of Patti, without any regard for the possible consequences to their voices.

The 'Method' provided Mrs Shaw with a creed and a purpose in life: she sang herself, helped to organize concerts, and spent much of her time working with Lee, who eventually came to live with the Shaws and share their financial burdens. In consequence, Shaw was surrounded by music from his childhood onwards: Mozart, Beethoven, Verdi, and Gounod were regularly rehearsed in the Shaws' drawing-room in 33 Synge Street and branded deeply into his consciousness. Also Lee's theories, not only in regard to music but on the subject of always sleeping with one's windows open and eating wholemeal instead of white bread, made a deep impression on him. Best of all, his financial contributions enabled the Shaws to take a summer cottage by the sea. 'I had one moment of ecstatic happiness in my childhood when my mother told me that we were going to live in Dalkey.' That 'removal from the street in which I was born, half of it faced with a very unpicturesque field which was soon obscured by a hoarding plastered with advertisements, to Torca Cottage, high

Shaw (right) and one of his Dublin friends, Edward McNulty, in 1874

Dublin Bay, to which the Shaws escaped from their depressing Dublin home

on Dalkey Hill, commanding views of Dublin Bay from Dalkey Island to Howth Head and of Killiney Bay from the island to Bray Head, with a vast and ever-changing expanse of sea and sky far below and far above' almost made up for the tribulations of his schooling.

Shaw's schooling

'I hated school, and learnt there nothing of what it professed to teach . . . My school was conducted on the assumption that knowledge of Latin is still the be-all and end-all of education . . . The method of teaching was barbarous: I was ordered to learn the declensions and conjugations and instalments of the vocabulary by rote on pain of being caned or "kept in" after school hours if I failed to reel off my paradigms without prompting . . . I escaped from my classical school just as Homer was threatening, but not before I was confronted with algebra without a word of the explanation that would have made it interesting to me.'

For a boy who, when still wearing dresses, had objected to the Catechism because he had to answer 'N or M', for no known reason, when asked his name, such schools were a stultifying waste of time.

But one particular school, the Central Model Boys' School in Marlborough Street, was a source of shame as well as discomfort. The Shaws belonged to the

Protestant minority in Dublin—a minority which counted itself infinitely and eternally superior to the Catholic masses; they were also 'gentlemen'; that is, they did not engage in trade or manual labour, even if they were constantly in debt. At this school, however, the majority of the boys came from Catholic tradesmen's homes: therefore boys of his own 'class' would not associate with Shaw outside school and inside it he would not associate with the boys around him. The experience was so humiliating that for eighty years he did not mention it to anyone, not even his wife. It was first divulged in his *Sixteen Self-Sketches*, published in 1949.

Eventually he was allowed to go back to a more bearable school and ended his career as a pupil in the Dublin English Scientific and Commercial Day School, an establishment which fitted boys for business.

First job   At fifteen he started work for an estate agent called Charles Uniacke Townshend. In his office, according to all reports, he was an excellent employee, accurate, efficient, and industrious; indeed, when the post of head cashier fell vacant he was promoted to it despite his youth. Moreover, most of his fellow-employees were University graduates, so that he had no feeling of social degradation. With them he discussed art, music, and literature after the doctrinaire fashion of youth and on one occasion Townshend was startled to hear, on entering the room, an impromptu rendering of an aria from *Il Trovatore*.

At home, however, matters were not improving. Mr Shaw was chronically incapable of maintaining his financial affairs on an even keel, or putting away the habit of drunkenness. In 1872 Lee left for London to seek greater opportunities, and Mrs Shaw, with typical energy, decided that her own career as a singing-teacher and her elder daughter Lucy's as a singer depended on their being near him. She abruptly sold the house and with the proceeds moved herself and her two daughters to England, where shortly afterwards Elinor Agnes (the younger of the two) died, evoking, Shaw said, the only display of maternal affection he had ever seen in his mother. She left her son and husband behind for practical reasons: the one because he was doing so well at Towns-hend's, the other because he was doing so badly at his own business. Ironically enough, she found, soon after her arrival in London, that Lee had abandoned his ideals and was advertising that he could create virtuosity in twelve-lesson courses. Without the slightest emotion she dropped his acquaintance after having sat at his feet for so many years.

Chichester Bell   For five years Shaw lived with his father in lodgings in Harcourt Street, where a fellow-lodger was Chichester Bell, the inventor of a phonetic script of the kind that Shaw came to champion years later. It was Bell who introduced Shaw to Wagner's music-drama, a subject on which he became enthusiastic and later wrote a book, *The Perfect Wagnerite*. Shaw acquired a good deal of information

Moody speaking at one of the revivalist meetings which he held with his fellow-evangelist, Ira Sankey. Shaw's letter about them which appeared in the *Public Opinion* was his first published work

in an unsystematic and rather solitary way: he frequented the theatre—where Barry Sullivan's power as an actor in an old-fashioned, heroic style captivated him—the concert hall, and the National Gallery of Ireland.

Finding himself suddenly bereft of music in the home, he taught himself to play the piano after a fashion, painfully picking out the notes of the overtures to Mozart's operas. But gradually he came to be more and more discontented with his life in the office and at home. The fact that in 1875 he contributed a page-long, hotly atheist letter to the Dublin Press on the subject of Moody and Sankey, the revivalists, shows that he was beginning to be pricked by a desire to make some kind of mark on the world. And when, in 1876, Mr Townshend placed his nephew over him in the office, despite Shaw's far better qualifications, it provided him with the final impetus. He resigned and left Dublin for his mother's home in Fulham. To the end, however, the firm thought well of him: there was no question of his being a failure as a clerk. Indeed, Mr Townshend wrote: 'Anything given him to do was always accurately and well done. We parted from him with regrets and shall always be glad to hear of his welfare.'

Shaw in 1876 with John Gibbings,
one of the other apprentices at
Mr Uniacke Townshend's office

Novel-writing

He went to London determined to make himself into a novelist. In the nineteenth century most of the greatest and most influential writers had been novelists; there had been Dickens, Thackeray, Eliot, Kingsley, Trollope. . . . It seemed to Shaw, as it has seemed to so many others before and since, that, with a little patient application, he must be able to succeed in this field. Every day he set himself to write five pages—no more, no less. 'I had so much of the schoolboy and the clerk still in me that if my five pages ended in the middle of a sentence I did not finish it until next day.' Again, many youths have adopted the same sort of programme; Shaw differed from them in that he actually completed five novels in this way, doggedly adding word to word, line to line, chapter to chapter. Each in turn was sent off to various publishers; each was returned as unsuitable and incompetent; and yet he pressed on with the next, often not knowing where he would find the postage to send it to yet another publisher.

Between his twenty-first and thirtieth year he earned virtually nothing and contributed nothing towards the household expenses, living entirely on his mother. Mr Shaw sent her £1 or 30s. from Ireland and she was able to draw on a legacy from her grandfather, but Shaw's boast, 'I did not throw myself into the struggle for life: I threw my mother into it', was very nearly true. He never abandoned his ambition to become a writer; while their flat (now in Fitzroy Square) echoed to his mother's music lessons and his sister Lucy's exercises, sung in preparation for the magnificent career which was mistakenly predicted for her, he toiled at his novels, deliberately refused to do anything in the way of earning money, grew steadily seedier in appearance and seemed bound to become permanently unemployable. A few jobs came his way almost by accident: he 'ghosted' a few articles on music for Lee; and he was given employment for a short while in the offices of the Edison Telephone Company. Moreover, it would be untrue to say that he earned nothing from writing: an article on Christian names brought him 15s., the copy for an advertisement for a patent medicine £5, and a short poem 5s. All the many other articles he wrote were returned, like his novels.

The Shaw of these years was a trial to himself and everyone about him. He skulked about in a rusty black suit, his collar and cuffs so frayed that he had to snip off the fringes with scissors. Once, at night-time, a prostitute accosted him in Piccadilly; he was too diffident to be able to shake her off immediately, but

Shaw when he was twenty-three and had joined his mother in London

Shaw in his Jaeger all-wool suit

when they arrived under a street-lamp and she saw his dilapidated appearance —to drive the point home he shook out his empty purse—she disappeared with affronted rapidity. His shyness was such that he could hardly bear to face anyone outside his immediate circle and, to counteract it, he adopted a pugnacious and hectoring manner which added nothing to his attractions. When invited, as a fellow-Dubliner, to a few of Lady Wilde's fashionable soirées, he must have presented a pitiful contrast with her poised and elegant son Oscar. He hated these experiences and swore each time never to go again.

To add to his awkwardness, he had already acquired many of the peculiarities for which he became noted later on, without any of the self-confidence necessary to carry them off. Shelley's works, all of which he had read, 'prose and verse from beginning to end', disgusted him with the 'savagery of a carnivorous diet', and in 1881 he became a vegetarian. This alone would have made him a difficult guest to entertain: during the day he champed his nut cutlets and supped his lentil soup in the newly opened vegetarian restaurants. Almost the first article of clothing he bought after years of painful shabbiness was an all-wool garment invented by Dr Jaeger and said to be more beneficial to health than the common garb of the day. 'I want my body to breathe,' he replied to those who

William Archer, one of the first friends
Shaw made in London

found the effect hideous. He had started to grow his ginger beard during an attack of smallpox, and his face, pale and frighteningly determined, glowed out from its straggly growth like a sickly but self-assertive moon in a threatening sky.

His mother must have found it difficult to think of any social *milieu* into which he would ever fit, but after a few years he began to evolve a pattern of life which suited him. When not writing at home, picking out Wagner scores on the piano, or visiting the National Gallery or Hampton Court he spent most of his time in the Reading Room of the British Museum, where he might have been seen studying Marx's *Das Kapital* and the score of *Tristan und Isolde* alternately. The Reading Room has always been the resort of the single-minded, from cranks to society-transformers; Marx himself worked there. One day Shaw's peculiar mixture of studies was noticed by William Archer, a young Scot already working in journalism who was himself a fanatical admirer of a little-known Norwegian playwright called Ibsen. They became friendly and, through Archer, Shaw was engaged to review several books for the *Pall Mall Gazette* at two guineas a thousand words. In 1885, the year when Shaw's father died and the family ceased to receive any money from that source, Archer was asked to become art critic for the *World*. He knew, and (what was more) admitted that

William Archer

Karl Marx

he knew, nothing about painting. Shaw, the *habitué* of the National Galleries of Ireland and England, guided his new friend round various art-collections and 'improved his mind' until he was able to write criticisms which resembled sense. He sent Shaw half the fee he was paid for them, but Shaw, poverty-stricken and thoroughly dependent as he was, refused to take it, saying that he did not originate the ideas he gave Archer; they were merely suggested to him by the pictures. Seeing that he would be obstinate in this matter and knowing how much he really needed the money, Archer told the Editor of the *World* that his article had really been written by Shaw. The post of art critic was offered to Shaw in place of Archer, and thus he was, almost unwillingly, eased into regular journalism. In his first year he earned exactly £117 0s. 3d.

Art critic

In a sense, then, his career as a journalist began as a result of his interest in Karl Marx. How had it come about that the snobbish, middle-class Shaw, who had been so distressed by the Central Model School, whose chief interests had been the gentle arts of music, painting, and literature, had become a Socialist and agitator for reform?

It was in 1879 that a friend, James Lecky, took him to the Zetetical Society, an *avant-garde* group which concerned itself with questions of reform, liberty,

Henry Mayers Hyndman,
the founder of the Democratic Federation,
one of the early Socialist organizations

and so forth. During the meeting he, who had never before spoken in public,
forced himself to make a speech and so disgraced himself, he felt, by his
nervousness and lack of skill that from then onwards he took every opportunity
of debating—at the Zetetical Society itself, the Browning Society, the Shakespeare
Society, everywhere possible—until he had forged himself into a fine orator who
was never at a loss for impromptu repartee.

At the beginning, the very thought of opening his mouth was a torture to *Learning to speak*
him. His heart pounded, the notes he had carefully prepared swam before his
eyes and he was convinced that, however incontrovertible his argument, it
would make no impression whatever. But with practice the nervousness began
to disappear. More important still, in 1884 he acquired a creed, a solid foundation
on which to build, and this gave him the confidence that comes of belonging to
a group and knowing that there are some, however small a number, whole-
heartedly on one's side. It was in that year that he happened to hear Henry
George speak on Land Nationalization and the Single Tax. Inspired by this
idea he attempted to confute with it the Marxist Federation run by Henry
Mayers Hyndman, and was contemptuously told that a man who had not read
Marx's *Kapital* was in no position to give his views. He went away and read

Sidney and Beatrice Webb, the eminent sociologists, who were close friends of Shaw's from the early days of the Fabian Society

Fabian Society

the book; it amazed, convinced, and fired him. Socialism was the answer to the problems of society. With Sidney Webb, a man of his own age whom he had met at the Zetetical, he joined the newly formed Fabian Society.

The ideals and sympathies of Socialism had already taken root in England to a certain extent, with some 'advanced' thinkers if not with the masses who were its main concern. There were already two Socialist societies in existence, but one was led by Hyndman, a wealthy philanthropist who tended to sweep aside the practical details of his programme, and the other by William Morris, a brilliant poet and designer but a poor politician. What was needed at that time was system, documentation, and propaganda, the conversion of Socialism from a fancy idea into a feasible political doctrine. And this is what the Fabians, with their fact-filled tracts and systematic infiltration of party organizations and local government, chiefly provided.

The Webbs

The leading members were well qualified to combine revolutionary thinking with solid documentation. There were the Webbs, Sidney and his wife Beatrice, lifelong friends of Shaw and both of them fantastically hard-working, seemingly

The Webbs' house at 41 Grosvenor Road, where they held earnest, fact-filled dinner-parties which were attended by most of the leading Socialists and many other politicians and public figures

tireless in amassing economic information. Before her marriage Beatrice had worked in an East End sweat-shop in order to gain first-hand knowledge of conditions there; Sidney had the perfectly functioning visual memory which enables a man to learn by heart a page of a book merely by looking at it. In the course of their career they wrote many weighty and convincing tomes, of one of which Shaw wrote to Ellen Terry: '. . . . read the proof sheets of the Webbs' great book *Industrial Democracy* (doesn't it sound succulent?).'

They were a fascinating pair—Sidney small, with a large head, like Daniel Quilp, thorough, a magnificent Civil Servant; Beatrice beautiful, priding herself on her objectivity as to work but in many ways outstandingly conventional. The Webbs frequently acted as hosts to the rest of the Fabians, either in the country, where they usually took a house for the summer, or at their house in the Grosvenor Road. H. G. Wells gave an almost undisguised portrait of their earnest entertainments in *The New Machiavelli*.

As well as the Webbs there were Sydney Olivier, another Civil Servant who later became Secretary of State for India (Sidney Webb was made Colonial

Mrs Annie Besant

Secretary in 1929), Graham Wallas, and, of course, Shaw. Of the relative characters and functions of Webb, Shaw, and Wallas, Beatrice Webb wrote:

'Sidney is the organiser and gives most of the practical initiative, Graham Wallas represents morality and scrupulousness, Bernard Shaw gives the sparkle and flavour. Graham Wallas appeals to those of the upper and educated class who have good intentions: no one can doubt his candour, disinterestedness, enthusiasm and extreme moral refinement. Sidney insinuates ideas, arguments, programmes and organises the organisers. Bernard Shaw leads off the men of straw, men with light heads—would-be revolutionaries, who are attracted by his wit, his daring onslaughts and amusing paradoxes. He has also a clientèle among the cynical journalists and men of the world.'

There were also such flamboyant characters as Mrs Annie Besant, who blazed a fiery career through journalism, politics, advocacy of birth control and theosophy, and had been associated with Charles Bradlaugh, the dreaded atheist; Hubert Bland, a thoroughly conventional country gentleman, except that he was addicted to having more than one wife at a time; and his legitimate wife, Edith Nesbit, a genius amongst children's book writers. Later they were joined by H. G. Wells.

A Socialist demonstration in Dod Street, Limehouse on 27 September 1885

As far as Shaw was concerned, there was now no lack of opportunities for public speaking. As a known Socialist orator he was sought after by 'advanced' clubs and societies all over the country. He spoke everywhere, from street corners to drawing-rooms, from public-house bars to cultural institutes. Accepting fees from nobody, he stipulated only that he should be free to speak on whatever subject he chose, however controversial. On two occasions he was so controversial as to escape prison by a hair's breadth—once in Dod Street, down by the Docks, when the police closed in on the meeting, and again at the World's End in Chelsea.

In the intervals between his public appearances, which took place on an average three times a week, he worked hard on the Fabian Society's executive committee, using his literary skill to make the Fabian Tracts readable, sifting information, continually thrashing out problems with the other members. In the Fabian committee he served as a sort of peculiar peacemaker:

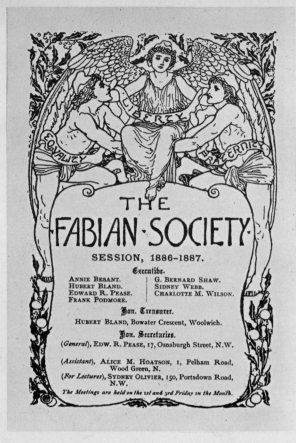

The Fabian Society
SESSION, 1886-1887.

Executive.

ANNIE BESANT.   G. BERNARD SHAW.
HUBERT BLAND.   SIDNEY WEBB.
EDWARD R. PEASE.   CHARLOTTE M. WILSON.
FRANK PODMORE.

Hon. Treasurer.

HUBERT BLAND, Bowater Crescent, Woolwich.

Hon. Secretaries.

(*General*), EDW. R. PEASE, 17, Osnaburgh Street, N.W.

(*Assistant*), ALICE M. HOATSON, 1, Pelham Road,
Wood Green, N.

(*For Lectures*), SYDNEY OLIVIER, 150, Portsdown Road,
N.W.

The Meetings are held on the 1st and 3rd Friday in the Month.

Title-page of the Fabian Society's
programme for 1886-7

'In the Fabian Cabinet, however, there was considerable strife of tempera-ments. . . . I believe that some of my own usefulness lay in smoothing out these frictions by an Irish sort of tact which in England seemed the most outrageous want of it. Whenever there was a quarrel I betrayed everybody's confidence by analysing it and stating it lucidly in the most exaggerated terms. Result: both sides agreed that it was all my fault. I was denounced on all hands as a reckless mischiefmaker, but forgiven as a privileged Irish lunatic.'

This was, however, the more peaceful side of Socialism. On at least one occasion the fight for better conditions was waged physically. There had been a rise in unemployment, and hence increased poverty, in the years leading up to 1887. In that year the police, irritated by the many marches and processions of unemployed men and 'political agitators', laid an embargo on meetings in Trafalgar Square. Shaw and his friends arranged a march for Sunday, 13th *'Bloody Sunday'* November, which afterwards they always referred to as 'Bloody Sunday'. He, William Morris, Annie Besant, Cunninghame-Graham, John Burns, Henry Salt, Edward Carpenter, and all the other 'stars' of the Socialist movement,

'Bloody Sunday'
(13 November 1887)
when a number of Socialists
and working-men who were
protesting against
unemployment were very
roughly treated by the police

proceeded at the head of crowds of working-men towards the Square. The protest met with complete disaster: they were cut off by troops of mounted policemen and cavalry, beaten back and, in many cases, roughly manhandled. Cunninghame-Graham was badly hurt and arrested (he spent his sentence in the prison hospital). Carpenter was clubbed by what he called 'that crawling thing, a policeman'. Salt had his watch stolen and, being of the anti-law party, could do nothing about it. The march ended in an ignominious retreat; it decided Shaw more strongly than ever that reform would be brought about by intellectual and political, rather than physical, pressure.

Henry Salt's sketch of his cottage at Tilford

The Salts

As a relaxation from the agitations and committees, the practical, fact-loving, no-nonsense Webbs and Oliviers, he could turn to another and quite different group of friends. Though they were also Socialists and probably seemed equally 'cranky' to the die-hards of the period, they believed in a return to a Rousseauesque simplicity rather than an extension of middle-class privileges. These were Henry Salt, who had given up a housemastership at Eton to live in a primitive cottage at Tilford, his wife Kate, his brother-in-law Jim Joynes, and Edward Carpenter, nicknamed by his friends 'the Noble Savage'. They wore sandals, honoured Shelley as a prophet, read poetry to each other and led a Spartan life which appealed to Shaw's Puritan side. With them he roamed about the Surrey countryside, 'staggering and slipping up and down places which Salt described as lanes, but which were, in fact, rapidly filling beds of mountain mud torrents', and enjoyed the experience of taking beauty with discomfort. With Kate he played long and extremely noisy arrangements of Wagner for four hands on the grand piano which was one of the few luxuries in the Tilford cottage. And always the conversation was diversified by heated discussions about the best way to solve social problems, the role of art, the proper sphere of Socialism.

Shaw reading the 'Song of the Respectables' to Salt   Mrs Jenny Patterson

But in some ways cracks were appearing in the solid structure of his Puritanism. 'I lived on pictures and music, opera and fiction, and thus escaped seduction until I was twenty-nine, when an enterprising widow, one of my mother's pupils, appealed successfully to my curiosity.' The fact is that, until the age of twenty-nine, he had neither the self-confidence nor the worldly advantages to approach girls, of his own class at least. Shabby, awkward, shy, a complete failure in all he had undertaken, he felt that no young woman could possibly view him with anything other than distaste. Suddenly Mrs Jenny Patterson, the 'pupil', showed him his mistake. It was no exaggeration to say that she seduced him; having done so, she pursued him so continuously and irksomely that he rebelled again and again. Like Julia in *The Philanderer*, for whom she was the model, she was of an extremely jealous temperament: scene followed scene, recriminations were heaped on recriminations; she dogged his footsteps, invaded his home, exploded into hysteria and generally made his life miserable.

Jenny Patterson

After this rather unhappy initiation, Shaw found himself with no lack of female company. In the nineties he met Florence Farr at a soirée of Morris's Socialist Society. She was a more amiable person than Jenny:

Florence Farr

'As she was clever, good-natured, and very good-looking, all her men friends fell in love with her. This had occurred so often that she had lost all patience with the hesitating preliminaries of her less practised admirers. Accordingly, when they clearly longed to kiss her, and she did not dislike them . . . she would seize the stammering suitor firmly by the wrists, bring him into her arms by a smart pull, and saying "Let's get it over", allow the gentleman to have his kiss and then proceed to converse with him at her ease on subjects of more general interest.'

Florence was entirely innocuous: better still, she was an actress and could benefit him in the theatrical way. Annie Besant, on the other hand, might have frightened a lesser man: she was given to worshipping idols and taking up creeds (the current one was Fabianism). In order to ingratiate herself with Shaw, she played interminable piano duets with him; as she was a very inferior

Florence Farr

Edith Nesbit (Hubert Bland's wife)

pianist, these were in the nature of epic battles. No doubt Mrs Besant brought to her struggles with crotchets and quavers the same indomitable energy with which she seasoned her fervent oratory and outraged Victorian convention. She did, however, allow Shaw to do art criticism for her magazine *Our Corner*, in which she also serialized his novels.

Edith Nesbit also 'had a crush on him', writing him innumerable poems and taking him for long and tiring walks; in fact, almost the only female Fabian who did not hanker after him at one time or another was the passionate but unsentimental Beatrice Webb, who declared that 'you cannot fall in love with a sprite and Shaw is a sprite in such matters, not a real person'.

All this adulation was a result of Shaw's Irish gallantry. Throughout his life he addressed most women, particularly if he wanted them to do something for him, in terms that suggested that he was besotted with love for them.

Irish gallantry

If they were sensible they accepted these high-flown tributes as lightly as they were given; if they were not, they accused Shaw of being nothing but a heartless philanderer.

William Morris and the Hammersmith Socialist League

Once, however, he himself was actually moved by a romantic impulse, in a fairy-tale, story-book way. He had spent a Sunday evening dining and lecturing at William Morris's enchanting house in Hammersmith, hung with delicately designed wallpapers and furnished with chairs and tables of medieval inspiration and great beauty.

'I was on the threshold of the Hammersmith house when I turned to make my farewell, and at this moment she came from the dining-room into the hall. [It was May Morris, the great designer's daughter.] I looked at her, rejoicing in her lovely dress and lovely self; and she looked at me very carefully and quite deliberately made a gesture of assent with her eyes. I was immediately conscious that a Mystic Betrothal was registered in heaven, to be fulfilled when all the material obstacles should melt away and my own position rescued from the squalors of poverty and unsuccess.'

But she 'married another' and although she afterwards divorced him, the Mystic Betrothal was never consummated.

Suddenly, from being a shy hobbledehoy, almost a recluse, with no occupation but his fruitless writing and no prospects before him, Shaw had become an extremely busy man, juggling mistresses, making dockside speeches and dealing expertly with hecklers, writing pamphlets and drafting reports, making plans to reform society and walking the Surrey hills with his 'simple-lifer' friends. Beatrice Webb summed him up, at this stage of his development, as 'fastidious but unconventional in his clothes; six feet in height with a lithe, broad-chested figure and laughing blue eyes. Above all a brilliant talker and, therefore, a delightful companion. . . . Some people would call him a cynic.' Sidney Webb, ironically watching his amorous exploits from respectable Grosvenor Road, observed: 'My! Shaw, you do warm both hands at the fire of life.'

By now he was truly launched on his career as a professional journalist. Far away from Hyde Park Corner or the Surrey hills, he was sweating, evening after evening, in crimson-plushed stalls at Covent Garden, having his ears blasted

May Morris

by healthy (if unskilled) lungs at Handel Festivals and sitting out solo recitals ranging from those of Clara Schumann and Adelina Patti at one end of the scale, to that of the 'Celebrated Lady Whistler' at the other. For from 1888 to 1890 he practised as music critic of the *Star* under the pseudonym of Corno di Bassetto, and from 1890 to 1894 held the same position on the *World*, under his own name.

He had been invited to join the *Star*, a Liberal journal, as a leader-writer, but the first articles he submitted to the Editor, T. P. O'Connor, were so enthusiastically Socialist that he was relieved of that post and relegated to the music criticism, where, it was thought, he could do no harm and could earn an honest two guineas a week. Music was generally held to be a mild, uncontroversial sphere of life and art, of interest to only a small minority. Shaw was never interested in appealing to small minorities. He determined to make his column a forum for the wider problems of art-attitudes in England. Confident in the knowledge that he had been surrounded by music since his earliest childhood, he charged on to the field of battle like a latter-day Voltaire, forcing interest with one hand, stripping away mystique with the other. As he was to do later in drama criticism, he made fun of all, or nearly all, the popular idols, the Drs Stanford, Parry, and Mackenzie; held up to ridicule the massed, white-gowned Handel Choirs and respectable but dull oratorios churned out by the dozen; laughed at the recitals of bloodless drawing-room ballads sung by virtuous but completely inartistic young ladies, and the virtuoso but mindless performances of Italian opera filling the repertoire at Covent Garden. Why, he demanded, was all this going on and attracting audiences, while Wagner, a composer worth ten of your Sullivans, Bellinis, and Brahmses, remained unperformed?

Whereas music critics before him had been solemn, sheeplike men, droning out boring technical descriptions of what they heard, he produced a column which anyone could understand and enjoy.

Musicians were outraged and maintained that he did not know what he was talking about; but general readers were entertained and took a fresh look at a subject which had previously been reserved for specialists. Many who had never before bothered with the musical column became regular followers of it and looked forward to each display of fireworks. But even so their circle was so small that Shaw was still a more or less unknown quantity as far as London was concerned, although by 1894 he was earning the munificent sum of £5 a week.

Here it may be said, very briefly, that the virtues of Shaw's music criticism were those of his non-dramatic writing in general: an extreme skill in creating a mood of comic detachment, by means of satire, irony, linguistic shock, and many other literary devices, so that readers were enabled to shed their acquired opinions and prejudices and look at various subjects with a completely fresh

Adelina Patti, one of the great virtuosi of the end of the last century

Shaw in the 1880's

eye. In this Shaw resembled the Voltaire of the *Dictionnaire Philosophique*: like the Frenchman, he was outstanding not so much because of what he said as because, by saying it, he made his readers think.

Frank Harris   During the nineties, he had come into contact with a buccaneering, rum, bustious journalist called Frank Harris over an article Shaw had written for the *Fortnightly Review*, of which Harris was then the Editor. Harris had pursued a rackety career all over the world, writing, editing, acting as a cowboy, hotel manager, and lawyer, and above all astounding most of his acquaintance with a Rabelaisian style of conversation, peppered with oaths and uproarious obscenities. Despite their great dissimilarity, the two men found common ground in their desire to see a more challenging kind of journalism than that generally practised: at their very first meeting Shaw exhibited a disregard for the conventions which made Harris warm to him. Harris had been describing how he had strained his heart when attempting to 'show off' in a boat. Shaw's rejoinder, instead of the polite sympathy expected, was a dispassionate question: 'Do you drink?'

As it happened, this was not one of Harris's intemperances, but the cool, objective way in which Shaw posed the question appealed to him as an Editor

Sarah Bernhardt

and towards the end of 1894, having bought the *Saturday Review*, he offered Shaw the post of drama critic at a salary of £6 a week. Edmund Yates, the Editor of the *World*, for whom Shaw was then writing music criticisms, had just died, so he felt it was an excellent opportunity to make a new start and conquer a fresh field. In 1895 he joined the *Saturday Review*.

From the moment when his first criticism (of Sydney Grundy's *Slaves of the Ring*) appeared, it was clear that a new and dominating personality, a one-man movement as it were, had appeared in the English theatrical world. It was, as Shaw later wrote, 'a siege laid to the theatre of the XIXth Century by an author who had to cut his own way into it at the point of the pen, and throw some of its defenders into the moat'. His bewildered readers found their most cherished idols under wholly irreverent attack. He laughed at Henry Irving, made jokes about Sarah Bernhardt, and even belittled the 'well-made play' then in vogue.

Even more shocking, he dared to criticize the Immortal Bard, William Shakespeare himself: 'How anybody over the age of seven can take any interest in a literary toy so silly in its conceit and common in its ideas as the Seven Ages of Man passes my understanding'; and one of Orlando's speeches: 'Was ever

A scene at a fashionable theatre in the 1890's

such canting, snivelling, hypocritical unctuousness exuded by an actor anxious to show that he was above his profession, and was a thoroughly respectable man in private life?'

This was brutal treatment of a public which had been brought up to revere Shakespeare, to worship him unquestioningly as a god. But for the first time it made people think who before had only believed, and impressed the new critic on their memories—as a man to be hated or a man to be admired, but always as a man with authority.

What his critics objected to most was this very tone of lofty, if kindly, detachment and his constant campaigning for a foreign modern playwright whom he actually compared with Shakespeare, to the English writer's disadvantage. Ibsen seemed to be an obsession with him: he condescendingly patted Eleonora Duse, the great Duse, on the head when she performed him, castigated old-established and admired managements like Irving's for not performing him, introduced his name on every possible occasion. If these critics

Ibsen

Henrik Ibsen

were exceptionally well-read they knew that in 1891 he had already published *The Quintessence of Ibsenism*, originally a lecture for the Fabians, in which he set out his reasons for admiring the Norwegian playwright. The fact was that he was postulating 'as desirable a certain kind of play in which I was destined ten years later to make my mark (as I very well foreknew in the depth of my own unconsciousness); and I brought everybody: authors, actors, manager and all, to the one test: were they coming my way or staying in the old grooves'.

Despite the authoritarian tone of the criticisms, Shaw's success as a playwright was still only a matter between himself and his 'unconsciousness'. By now he had, of course, completely given up the novelist idea and written five plays, but only two had been performed: one for two nights only and the other for eleven weeks, during which it made a loss of some £2,000.

The genesis of *Widowers' Houses* was peculiar. As early as 1885, when he was still reviewing odd books for the *Pall Mall Gazette*, and indeed only two years after his last attempt to write a novel, William Archer had suggested that they

Widowers' Houses'

The original programme for *Widowers' Houses*

should collaborate on a play; he would provide the plot and construction (he modelled the plot on Augier's *Ceinture Dorée*) and Shaw would provide the dialogue. After a short time Shaw coolly asked for more material, as he had used up the plot in the first two acts. He read them to Archer who fell asleep during the second act and on waking explained carefully that a plot could not be extended or varied in that fortuitous way. Meeting with only irreverent mockery of the 'cult of plots' in general, he then abandoned the whole project. Nor was he the only person to think poorly of Shaw's first dramatic effort. When appealed to for his opinion on the two acts, Henry Arthur Jones, one of the most popular playwrights of the day, paused thoughtfully and said: 'Where's your murder?'

The play was laid aside, unfinished. Even if it had been finished, there would have been no commercial theatre in which it could have been performed in London. Theatrical economics resembled those of today. Unadventurous managers of commercial theatres claimed that they could not afford to experiment because it cost so much to produce and stage a play that unless it was a huge popular success it would make a crippling loss. But fortunately in 1891 a

Jacob Grein, who founded the
Independent Theatre Society

Dutch Jew called Jacob Thomas Grein, who had a great love for the theatre
and a desire to inject a little new blood into its veins, founded a play-producing
concern called the Independent Theatre Society and proceeded to horrify the
London critics with his first production, 'an open drain; a loathsome sore
unbandaged' called *Ghosts*. It was put on at the Royalty Theatre in Soho, and
earned for Grein a huge *succès de scandale* with the host of the respectable and
the firm approval of the *avant-garde*, such as Shaw.

Grein's only difficulty was lack of material. In 1892 he confessed to Shaw
that, though he had made every attempt to do so, he had not been able to find
an English play of like seriousness to follow up *Ghosts*. Shaw suggested a play
by himself and hurriedly finished the now unrecognizable *Ceinture Dorée*,
adding a third act and revising throughout. It was produced in December 1892
for two nights only, with Florence Farr as Blanche Sartorius and James Welch
(who acted in several later Shaw plays) as Lickcheese. It was, of course, booed
by the devotees of the old school of drama, and the critics, who discussed it for
a fortnight, agreed that Shaw might be a forceful pamphleteer but was certainly
no playwright.

J. T. Grein

Shaw was so busy during the early years of his career that he did much
of his writing on the tops of buses like those shown here

But now that he had begun to write plays, Shaw knew instinctively that this
was his true talent. In between rushing from theatre to theatre, from Socialist
meeting to Fabian committee, from the International Socialist Congress to the
Wagner Festival at Bayreuth, he scribbled down dialogue wherever he happened
to be—mostly on the tops of buses and in underground trains. For this reason
he used scores of little notebooks which could be crammed into the pockets of
his Jaeger suit. He had the useful faculty of being able to make himself entirely
oblivious of his surroundings and switch from one kind of work to another
without pausing in between. This was fortunate, for during his short 'holidays'
from the grind of London critical life, when he stayed in the country with the
Webbs, they continued to make full use of him for the cause:

'Bernard Shaw [wrote Beatrice in her diary] has stayed with us the remainder
of our time working almost every morning at our book [*The History of Trade
Unionism*]. The form of the first chapter satisfied him, and he altered only words
and sentences. The second chapter he took more in hand and the third he has
to a large extent remodelled. Sidney certainly has devoted friends. But then it is
a common understanding with all these men that they use each other up when
necessary.'

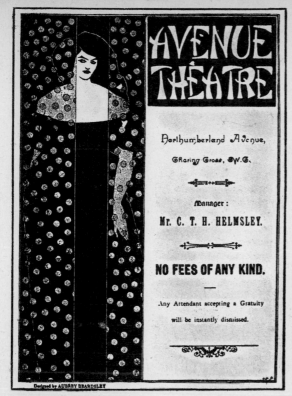

The programme for *Arms and the Man*   Alma Murray as Raïna in *Arms and the Man*

At the same time he was writing *The Philanderer*, a poor play showing two women (one based on the stormy Jenny Patterson) skirmishing over a man, against a background of Ibsenism, the movement fashionable amongst the *avant-garde* of the literary world. This play had to wait twelve years for its first public performance. The next, *Mrs Warren's Profession*, was not publicly performed until 1925: as its theme was the evils of a society which offered far greater rewards to a prostitute than to an honest working-woman, the Lord Chamberlain refused it a licence. However, a few years later Arnold Daly produced it in New York.

Shaw's first play to make any real impression on the public, *Arms and the Man*, written in 1894, was considerably more conventional. It was produced in that year at the Avenue Theatre by Florence Farr in a season of new plays financed by Miss Emma Horniman, a moderately wealthy Quaker, who, unusually, applied her benevolence to the theatre.

This time Shaw had set about debunking contemporary literature. In place of the conventional heroic soldier of the day, he presented a soldier who, though efficient, admitted to cowardice and to keeping up his courage by eating chocolates on the battlefield. Instead of the conventional Ruritanian young lady

'Arms and the Man'

of noble blood he showed a girl who was a termagant and a liar. Instead of the conventional devoted manservant he showed one who was only interested in making the maximum out of his employers in order to start his own business.

During rehearsal the actors completely failed to understand what it was all about; consequently on the first night they played it as a serious piece and were received with roars of delighted laughter. Unfortunately this convinced them that it was, after all, meant to be a comedy and from the second night they played it 'for laughs', with the result that its ironic humour fell flat and the play had to be taken off after eleven weeks. However, the first night at least had been a huge success; only one hiss was heard amongst a storm of applause. Shaw, taking his call, bowed in the direction of this hiss and said: 'I quite agree with you, sir, but what can two do against so many?'

Nevertheless, even if *Arms and the Man* failed to revitalize London comedy overnight it made a small stir and later Shaw managed to give it joking publicity in the *Saturday Review*: 'I find other critics . . . declaring that *The Importance of Being Earnest* is a strained effort of Mr Wilde's at ultra-modernity, and that it could never have been written but for the opening up of entirely new paths in drama by *Arms and the Man*.' Moreover, it was at least successful in impressing Richard Mansfield, a popular American actor-manager, who bought the American rights and produced the play frequently in the United States, which thenceforth became, at least partially, aware that Shaw existed.

In 1893 and 1894, in between criticisms, he had paid hurried visits to Florence and other parts of Italy to study 'the religious art of the Middle Ages and its destruction by the Renascence'. On the whole he decided that the artistic situation in England was healthier. He had 'hurried back to Birmingham to discharge my duties as musical critic at the Festival there'. In that city 'a very remarkable collection of the works of our British "pre-Raphaelite" painters was on view. I looked at these, and then went into the Birmingham churches to see the windows of William Morris and Burne-Jones. . . . The art it had to show me was the work of living men whereas modern Italy had as far as I could see no more connection with Giotto than Port Said has with Ptolemy.'

He decided that his next play should show Pre-Raphaelitism being challenged by something stronger still. Putting the memories of the other play-fiascos behind him, he began on *Candida*.

'*Candida*'

It met with a mixed reception even from his friends. When he stayed with the Webbs in the country, the party usually worked at some sociological writing in the morning, cycled in the afternoon, and spent the evening listening to Shaw reading his latest play—probably constituting the most sympathetic of his audiences. But when Beatrice Webb heard *Candida*, she called its heroine a 'sentimental prostitute'. Edward Carpenter said: 'No, Shaw, it won't do.' Kate

Shaw in the 1890's

Salt, on whom he had partly based the character of Candida, did not care for it. George Alexander, to whom Shaw offered the play, thought the poet's part would not gain the sympathy of the audience. But Ellen Terry, on the other hand, was deeply moved: 'I've cried my eyes out over your horrid play, your *heavenly* play . . . I must keep my blue glasses on all the while for my eyes are puffed up and burning.' In the end none of the commercial managers he offered it to accepted it and, with the exception of two provincial tours and a semi-amateur performance in London, it was not seen until 1904.

The time had come to take stock of himself. His exploits in public speaking were all very well, but they were not adding anything to his theatrical prestige and took his attention away from more important things. From his music and drama criticisms he knew the general character of his talent: he was a superb publicist, a writer who, by tackling with his own particular wit and readability subjects which had previously been considered dull and specialized, could make them a matter of general concern. And he was convinced that he also knew his specific talent, playwriting.

Edward Carpenter

George Alexander

To clear his mind about his attitude to art in general he wrote *The Sanity of Art*. This was a reply to Dr Max Nordau's *Entartung*, a psychological treatise full of important-sounding terms like 'the non-ego' and 'the elaboration of the motor impulses', on the innate degeneracy of art and artists, with particular reference to such men as Tolstoy and Wagner, Rossetti and Verlaine, the Pre-Raphaelites and the Decadents, Nietzsche and Ibsen. Shaw's reply was not especially distinguished; it was heated, biased, and deliberately subjective, like all his 'scholarly' work. But at least it proclaimed, once and for all, his conception of the artist as a crusader, reformer, world-leader—everything that is least decadent. He was never interested in art for its own sake but only for the good that it could do—not necessarily by advocating measures of one kind or another but by clarifying the intellect and ennobling the soul. Mere sensual enjoyment had little appeal for him: this is why Chesterton called him a Puritan.

Having made his point, he tried once again to force an entrance into the professional theatre, this time setting his sights on the highest target of all. *The*

Man of Destiny, one of the two plays of 1895, was written as a bravura piece for two actors (there are virtually only two parts in it: Napoleon and the Strange Lady). Shaw intended it for either Mansfield or Irving and he definitely wanted Ellen Terry to play the Strange Lady, but once again he was to be disappointed: Mansfield found the part uncongenial and Ellen, who was under contract to Irving, could never appear in it because Irving himself could not be brought to make a definite decision about the matter until it was too late.

Ellen Terry

Shaw had begun to correspond with Ellen Terry three years earlier. She had asked him, as music critic of the *World*, to give his opinion on a young singer of her acquaintance. He replied with a detailed discussion of the advantages and disadvantages of music as a career for the girl, and from that time onwards they wrote to each other at longer or shorter intervals almost until Ellen Terry's death. It was a curious correspondence. Shaw was on the verge of a stormy but eventually triumphant career; Ellen was nearing the end of a lifetime on the stage, where she had been universally loved for her sweetness, good sense, loyalty, and complete lack of jealousy or cruelty. Shaw, revolutionary and outrageous, would stop at nothing, not even harsh treatment of Irving, to promote his new and very un-Irvingesque drama; Ellen, though she admired Shaw and was too intelligent not to feel the force of much that he said, loved Irving and hated to hurt him, even when he was being palpably unfair to her. Yet for years these two opposites sustained a sort of epistolary infatuation; or rather, Shaw poured out a passion and gallantry which he could best sustain on paper while Ellen returned him the loving benevolence which she bestowed on all her acquaintances.

Irving

Irving was in the line of the great actor-managers, or actor-producers, of the past: the Burbages, Keans, and Macreadys. His personality and acting powers were so forceful that audiences were hypnotized by whatever he played, from Shakespeare to trite melodrama. Shaw had admired his performance in *Two Roses* many years earlier in Ireland; most critics, including Archer, had been enraptured by his super-intelligent re-creation of Shakespearean characters which for years past had been merely vehicles for loud shouting and over-acting; he took infinite trouble over the production, scenic design, and presentation of the plays he put on; and he waged an unceasing battle for the recognition of acting as a fine art and the death of the old legend that actors were, by definition, immoral and beyond the pale of decent society. He and Shaw thus had many aims in common; why did Shaw make such a concentrated onslaught on him from the moment he became drama critic on the *Saturday Review*? Chiefly, of course, because Shaw, as a playwright, was bound to be affronted by the kind of actor who makes the audience oblivious to the quality of the play in their admiration of the player; partly because Irving was wasting Ellen Terry's enormous talent and charm on trivial 'vehicles' and supporting parts.

Ellen Terry, with whom Shaw had a long and endearing correspondence although most of his theatrical plans for her came to nothing

Max Beerbohm's cartoon of
Henry Irving as a 'man
of distinction'

'The Man of Destiny'

The great anti-Irving campaign had already started when Shaw told Ellen that he had 'just finished a beautiful little one-act play for Napoleon and a strange lady'. Ellen was intrigued by the idea, entranced by the play itself, and eager for Irving and herself to perform it. Without consulting Shaw, she showed it to Irving and reported back that 'H.I. quite loves it and will do it finely.'

Even though Ellen gave a warning that a one-act play was always difficult to fit into a programme, anyone else would have been transported with joy at the mere possibility of the performance taking place. Shaw's first reaction was quite different. It had been a common practice for actor-managers to buy up drama critics' plays without any intention of ever performing them, thus transferring a surreptitious bribe to the critic and ensuring glowing notices for themselves; Irving himself had been guilty of this in the past. Now, no sooner had the question of Irving's interest been raised than Shaw, priding himself as usual on his clear-sightedness, leaped to the suspicion that Irving's intentions were dishonourable. Before any offer had been made, he began displaying his principles to Ellen: 'As long as I remain a dramatic critic I can neither sell

Arthur Conan Doyle

plays nor take advances. I must depend altogether on royalties and percentages on actual performances. Otherwise, you see, I should simply be bribed right and left . . .' and so forth, in a tone of righteous, but as yet quite unnecessary, protestation.

Irving read the play, a dialogue between Napoleon and a lady whom he encountered during the campaigns of 1796. It was wordy, he thought; it contained a long, satirical description of the English character as seen by Napoleon; but it would do. In July 1896 he offered Shaw £50 a year for the rights in the play, together with his promise that he would perform it as soon as he was able—terms which Conan Doyle, already the best-selling author of the Sherlock Holmes stories, had been very glad to accept for *his* one-act play.

'To this [wrote Shaw sternly to Ellen] I replied by proposing three alternatives. 1. My original conditions (virtually). 2. That you should have the play to amuse yourself with until you were tired of it without any conditions at all. 3. That he should have a present of it on condition of his instantly producing works by Ibsen.'

Henry Irving as Richard III

Irving, understandably, was disinclined to bother with the vagaries of this young crank and allowed the matter to lapse. In September Shaw returned to the attack. Irving had announced that his theatre, the Lyceum, would present *Madame Sans-Gêne*, a play by Sardou which also had Napoleon as its hero. Shaw asked if this ruled out the possibility of performing his play and received what he called a 'summons' to see Irving in person. The interview went badly: 'I like Henry', wrote Shaw loftily, 'though he is without exception absolutely the stupidest man I ever met.' It was inevitable that he and Irving should never be joined in collaboration; it almost seemed that Shaw was doing his utmost to antagonize the actor. Of his performance in *Richard III* he wrote: 'In the heavy singlehanded scenes . . . he was not, as it seemed to me, answering his helm satisfactorily. . . . He made some odd slips in the text. . . . In the tent and battle scenes his exhaustion was perhaps too genuine to be quite acceptable as

Quarrel with Irving

part of the play.' Irving's henchmen sprang to the conclusion that this was an accusation of drunkenness; to them the Chief was not only a great actor but a model of all the virtues, a sacrosanct, almost churchman-like figure against whom such imputations were sacrilege. When Shaw, hearing of the error, wrote to Irving that he had had no such idea in his head, the great man was foolish enough to reply that he 'had not the privilege of reading your criticism'.

This brush, a suggestion in the Press that Irving had sent back *The Man of Destiny* to 'teach him better manners' and an official note from Bram Stoker, Sir Henry's *aide*, saying that he had changed his mind about producing the play, inspired Shaw to attack again. 'I am spoiling for a row . . .' he wrote to Ellen. 'Watch the fun and chuckle. Leave them to me. Hahah!!!' Ellen's loving concern for both parties achieved no result in the end, beyond the fact that in the years to come Irving began to doubt her loyalty. On this occasion she tried her hardest to bring Irving and Shaw together, the sweetness of her nature being shown in her: 'My chief desire in the affair is that *he* plays the part, for it's a part to play! For both your sakes I desire this.' But it was no good. There were more angry exchanges between Irving and Shaw, Irving maintaining that he could not name a specific date for a production of the play, Shaw accusing him of bad faith. The idea of the bribe was still in Shaw's mind, and Irving, as Ellen said, 'don't think the whole thing matters much'. *The Man of Destiny* was never produced or acted by Irving and Ellen Terry: it first reached the London stage under the direction of Granville-Barker. Irving's final comment was that he would willingly pay Shaw's funeral expenses at any time.

Margaret Halston as the Strange
Lady in the first production of
The Man of Destiny

In 1899 Ellen Terry showed Irving the script of *Caesar and Cleopatra* but he was not interested in it, even though the part of Caesar would have suited him. In 1900 she tried again with *Captain Brassbound's Conversion*; once again Irving demurred, remarking that the play reminded him of a comic opera. The part of Lady Cicely Wayneflete was written by Shaw specially for Ellen; it was also intended to be a dramatic re-creation of her character, although at first she found this hard to believe: 'It's not the sort of play for me in the least . . . Mrs Potter would revel in the part, but it is surely for Mrs Pat. *Not* for me . . . it would not "Act well".'

This was a blow which really hurt Shaw. After all their sympathetic correspondence, the way in which Ellen had grasped the meaning of his suggestions and criticisms about her acting and drama in general, and their conspiracies over *The Man of Destiny* and *Caesar and Cleopatra*, it seemed like the desertion of Brutus when even she failed to appreciate his efforts.

Eventually Ellen came to think better of the play, although she doubted whether it would be a commercial success, but her commitments, first to Irving and then to others, prevented her from playing it until 1906, when it was produced at the Court Theatre under the Vedrenne-Barker management. By that time she was already elderly; although she took immense pains over her part, studying each detail with the completely selfless humility which she never lost, the Shaw-Terry combination was not the great success which might have been expected.

Ellen Terry as Lady Cicely Wayneflete in
Captain Brassbound's Conversion

H. G. Wells in the 1890's

To return to 1895; the fate of Shaw's other play of that year, *You Never Can Tell*, was probably even more frustrating than that of *The Man of Destiny*. Despite the fact that George Alexander had said, after reading it, 'When I got to the end I had no more idea what you meant by it than a tom cat', it was put into rehearsal at the Haymarket in 1897. However, soon afterwards it was withdrawn because the actors found it unactable. And this was a play in which he had sacrificed his reforming ideals, an 'acting' play, a play in which he had for once attempted to woo the wider public!

The theatre was a fickle jade: at least politics and sociology could be trusted to follow predictable lines; at least he was appreciated by the Fabians. He continued to be a stalwart member of the Society, as useful in committee and active in drafting documents as ever, and maintained his close friendship with the Webbs, spending frequent working holidays with them in the country. When staying with them at Beachy Head he learned to ride a bicycle. Moreover in 1895 he met H. G. Wells for the first time, an encounter which was to lead to a lifelong

'You Never Can Tell'

The St Pancras Town Council in 1900. Shaw is at the front of the right-hand table

friendship, diversified by several differences of opinion, particularly where the policy of the Fabian Society was concerned. In 1897 he became a vestryman of St Pancras (the London vestries were later joined up to form boroughs) and for the next six years proved a very able and untemperamental councillor, working happily side by side with tradesmen, bank managers, and Methodist ministers, rarely trying to show off and always eager to take his share of the work. He served on several committees and, as one of his biographers, R. F. Rattray, says, 'was a pioneer in providing public lavatories for women'.

With all this, he managed to finish *The Devil's Disciple*—'three acts, six scenes, a masterpiece, all completed in a few weeks, with a trip to Paris and those Ibsen articles thrown in—articles which were so overwritten that I cut out and threw away columns. Not to mention the Bradford election.' He had written the main part for William Terriss, a highly successful actor of the day, but was once again thwarted, this time by the untimely assassination of Terriss by a madman. However, the play was produced in New York by the faithful

Richard Mansfield as
Dick Dudgeon in
The Devil's Disciple

Richard Mansfield and proved to suit the American taste of that year to such an extent that, although it was not produced in the West End until nine years later, in 1898 Shaw was able to give up his post on the *Saturday Review* and devote himself entirely to playwriting and free-lance work.

But 1898 was remarkable for another occurrence besides the production of *The Devil's Disciple*. When staying with the Webbs at Saxmundham two years earlier, Shaw had written to Ellen:

'This time we have been joined by an Irish millionairess who has had cleverness and character enough to decline the station of life—"great catch for somebody"—to which it pleased God to call her, and whom we have incorporated into our Fabian family with great success. I am going to refresh my heart by falling in love with her . . . but, mind, only with her, not with the million; so someone else must marry her if she can stand him after me.'

The millionairess was Miss Charlotte Payne-Townshend, then thirty-nine. Before long Shaw has changed his tack and is telling Ellen that 'I have got

Charlotte
Payne-Townshend

to like her so much that it would be superfluous to fall in love with her', and a few months later he is lightly proposing to 'treat her to a stall (cant very well take a millionairess to the pit)'. But then he lost confidence, as he confided to Ellen, at the same time giving a sketch of the lady's character:

'She doesnt really *love* me. The truth is, she is a clever woman. She knows the value of her unencumbered independence, having suffered a good deal from family bonds and conventionality. . . . The idea of tying herself up again by a marriage before she knows anything—before she has exploited her freedom and money power to the utmost—seems to her intellect to be unbearably foolish. . . .'

Shaw was being cautious. On the one hand, the lady's wealth bothered him; throughout his life he tended to preach revolution and practise convention, and the thought of marrying her without a prospect of financial success was intolerable to him. On the other hand, he was, one feels, saving his face in advance by a show of mock modesty and frivolity, as he was to do many times again. Ellen, with her directness and open-hearted generosity, would have none of this. 'How very silly you clever people are. Fancy not knowing! Fancy not being sure!' But it seemed for a while as if the affair would come to nothing: '. . . and now, dear Ellen, she is a free woman, and it has not cost her half a farthing, and she has fancied herself in love, and known secretly that she was only taking a prescription, and been relieved to find the lover laughing at her and reading her thoughts.'

But the relief was only temporary. Soon Ellen was inviting Shaw to bring the lady round to her dressing-room after the play and Shaw was hotly refusing: 'She is not cheap enough to be brought round to your room and *shewn* to you. She isnt an appendage, this green-eyed one, but an individual.'

References to 'Miss P.T.' came thick and fast: to her cycling with the Fabians in the country, to her flat in London, to her acting as secretary for Shaw, to her rubbing a 'bicycle gash in my cheek with vaseline in the hope that diligent massage might rub it out and restore my ancient beauty', to Shaw's 'genius for hurting women . . . always . . . with the best intentions'. Shaw, always an active and tireless walker, bustled her round the countryside of Wales, Suffolk, or Sussex according to where they happened to be staying. At first 'she used to stop in five minutes and get palpitations and say I must not walk like an express train. Now she hooks on and steeplechases with me without turning a hair.'

And at last there were no more doubts as to their mutual affection and suitability. Moreover by now (1898) the proceeds from *The Devil's Disciple* made Shaw feel that their financial positions might well become less ludicrously unequal. Matters were precipitated when he fell ill from overwork and an accident which caused necrosis of the bone in one of his feet. At that time he was

A scene from the 1907 production of *The Devil's Disciple*

still living in Fitzroy Square with his mother, who cared little or nothing for the comforts, let alone the graces, of home life. Charlotte was horrified by the condition in which she found him: his room was so cluttered with books and papers, each placed open on top of the next, that the servants left it severely alone and he was languishing amidst dust, disorder, and the cold, congealed remains of meals which had not been taken away. She invited him to stay at her house in the country and be properly looked after, but Shaw, again with surprising regard for the *qu'en-dira-t-on*, refused to do so unless they were man and wife.

The couple, both over forty, were married in 1898 and took up residence in Charlotte's flat in Adelphi Terrace over the Webbs' new foundation, the London School of Economics. The actual ceremony was as disconcerting to all parties as all Shaw's attempts at normality. He looked so disreputable as he walked in on his crutches (he used them for eighteen months) and Graham Wallas, one of his witnesses, looked so distinguished in his best clothes that the registrar concluded that the latter must be the bridegroom, taking Shaw 'for the inevitable beggar who completes all wedding processions'. Such, at least, was Shaw's description of the occasion.

Marriage

Despite this inauspicious beginning the marriage lasted very happily until the end of the Shaws' lives. Both were comfortable and Charlotte, who was all that is most unlike temperamental, over-emotional theatre people and politicians,

Adelphi Terrace, where Charlotte had a flat

provided a soothing haven to which Shaw could withdraw after his battles, besides spurring him on to make journeys abroad which he hated in anticipation but enjoyed in the doing.

Charlotte was a curious woman. She was by no means unintelligent, did a certain amount of writing and translating, interested herself in the Fabians and economic theory, endowed a scholarship for women at the London School of Economics and, towards the end of her life, became absorbed in religious matters. She fitted like the last piece of a jigsaw puzzle into the Webbish, earnest side of Shaw's life, the Puritan rather than the flamboyant side. 'I wonder what you would think of our life,' he had written to Ellen in 1897, 'our eternal political shop; our mornings of dogged writing, all in separate rooms; our ravenous plain meals; our bicycling; the Webbs' incorrigible spooning over their industrial and political science; Miss P.T., Irish, shrewd and green-eyed, finding everything "very interesting"; myself always tired and careworn and always supposed to be "writing to Ellen". You'd die of it all in three hours, I'm afraid.'

Charlotte Shaw

Shaw, instead of dying of it, came more and more to accept it as the only reality. 'What people call love,' he wrote to Ellen Terry, 'is impossible except as a joke . . . between two strangers meeting accidentally at an inn or in a forest path. . . . A delusion, Ellen, all this love romance: that way madness lies.' Romance, sentiment, the love which is not mere affection and liking, belonged to plays, to correspondences like that with Ellen, to evanescent affairs (like his early ones with Jenny Patterson and Florence Farr or the later encounter with Mrs Patrick Campbell) which were never intended to last or leave a permanent mark, which could be closed and written off as brief escapes into a fantasy, non-real world.

Shaw on love

When, much later, Mrs Patrick Campbell, to whom passion *was* a reality, tried to drag such an incident into the real world of books, publishers, contracts, and Charlotte, Shaw felt that he was being attacked below the belt and resented it strongly. Perhaps if Charlotte had been a warmer woman, Shaw's own personality might have lost that lack of interest in feelings which sometimes made him callous to the feelings of others, but warmness was foreign to her

Shaw in about 1901

nature. She was not fond of children: indeed she was firmly resolved against bearing them or entering into sexual relations at all. St John Ervine surmises that this was the reason for the ending of her earlier love affair with Axel Munthe, the Swedish writer. At any rate, Shaw contented himself with what he had, although he was well aware that it was incomplete: 'What can childless people with independent incomes, marrying at forty as I did, tell you about marriage? I know nothing about it except as a looker-on.'

'Caesar and Cleopatra'

Although from now on Shaw had a more settled home-life, his ventures in the theatre continued to meet with little success. In 1898, while still hobbling about on crutches, he wrote *Caesar and Cleopatra*, intending the main roles for Mrs Patrick Campbell and Johnston Forbes-Robertson, the actor who was succeeding to Irving's position as national idol. Once again he failed to find favour: Forbes-Robertson claimed that he could not run the risk of such an expensive production. Irving, as aforesaid, did not care for the play. Nobody, except Ellen Terry, who could not play it, seemed to have confidence in this debunking of the traditional 'historical spectacular' with its incredibly heroic

Johnston Forbes-Robertson as Caesar in
Caesar and Cleopatra

heroes and heroines. Yet its Caesar (small, bald, refusing the 'correct' heroisms of revenge and passionate love) and its Cleopatra (childish, bad-mannered, and spiteful) are perfect parts for actors to play, and the whole conception, that of an immensely powerful man educating an attractive but unformed girl, is surely as erotic as the same situation in *Pygmalion*, which was an immediate success with everybody.

Shaw, now forty-two, decided that, since almost nobody was willing to perform his plays, he would publish them in book-form. In 1898 he set out to prepare *Plays Pleasant and Unpleasant* (comprising *Widowers' Houses*, *The Philanderer*, *Mrs Warren's Profession*, *Arms and the Man*, *Candida*, *The Devil's Disciple*, and *You Never Can Tell*) for press. As usual, having embarked on an enterprise for pragmatical reasons, he gave it all the urgency of a mission, dogmatizing about typography and bindings, insisting on a certain type, on the use of spaced letters for emphasis instead of italics. This is a clumsy method, as one-letter words still have to be italicized and spaced-out short words are not very noticeable, but, having committed himself to it, Shaw made it an

Author and publisher

The Relief of Ladysmith, one of the most emotional moments in a highly emotional war

article of faith like his omission of the apostrophe in words like 'can't' and his simplified spellings. He used his publisher only as a distributor, himself giving directions to the printers, binders, typographers, and paper-merchants and paying them directly. Moreover he read all the proofs himself, treasuring each comma and colon like a favourite child and making numerous emendations, on the first proofs at least. He acted as his own agent, commissioning his own translators abroad, dealing with infringements of copyright, haggling about terms with anyone who wanted to produce any of his material. In general he prided himself on his clear-sightedness in matters of business; his suspicion of publishers equalled his earlier suspicion of Irving. 'Let nothing induce you to accept a publisher's contract without expert advice,' he warned Mrs Patrick Campbell some years later: '*all* publishers' contracts are booby traps.'

The Boer War The first year of Shaw's married life coincided with the outbreak of the Boer War, which marked the virtual end of the confident, unshakeable Victorian era, and raised doubts in many minds. It divided opinion through-out Britain, almost regardless of political party. As Beatrice Webb wrote: 'The cleavage goes right through the Liberal Party into the Fabian Society, Shaw, Wallas and Whelen being almost in favour of the [Boer] war, J. R. Macdonald

Shaw's Corner at Ayot St Lawrence

and Sydney Olivier desperately against it, while Sidney occupies a middle position.' By and large, the conventional anti-reactionaries came out strongly on the side of the Boers—the little nation brutally attacked by big, powerful Britain.

Not for the first or last time, Shaw's reaction was completely individual and unexpected. While deploring the financial interests which led many to advocate the war, he nevertheless joined their side, on the grounds that the Empire could pave the way to internationalism, whereas the nationalism of South Africa could only lead to enormous power being placed in the hands of a small and exceptionally bigoted community. In 1900 he finished *Fabianism and the Empire*, ostensibly the product of the whole Fabian Society but in fact written by him alone. It caused the split described by Beatrice Webb and left the emotional anti-imperialists, all sympathy and unreflecting sentiment, open-mouthed.

In 1905 the Shaws, after having rented various country houses for short periods, finally settled down into permanent respectability at Ayot St Lawrence in Hertfordshire (they kept on the London flat). Their house there was not particularly handsome; but it was solid and conventional, like the life which Charlotte endeavoured to create for her husband. She had done her best to

Ayot St Lawrence

The house in Fitzroy Square
where Shaw lived with his mother
until his marriage. Charlotte was
horrified by the squalid conditions
she found here

detach him from the peculiar friends of his earlier days—the Noble Savage, Graham Wallas, Henry Salt, and the rest. Before his marriage Kate Salt had for some time acted as his secretary, going daily to Fitzroy Square, typing out his lectures, articles, plays, and criticisms, and by way of relaxation playing Wagner on the piano while he sang in a lusty baritone. However, as soon as Charlotte appeared on the scene she banished Kate, as a relic of former days, and indeed forbade her entrance to the house.

Shaw no longer worked amid dust and litter. On the contrary, all his meals were served up on time, his study was kept swept and dusted, he was relieved of all domestic cares. He had a sort of summer-house in the garden in which he could work completely free from interruption and almost in the open air. It also enabled his wife to say, without an absolute lie, that he was 'out' to any caller whom she thought undesirable.

By the early years of the century the name Shaw was beginning, slowly, to be heard abroad. *Caesar and Cleopatra* was given a spectacular production at the Neues Theater in Berlin; various other plays were put on in Vienna, Leipzig,

Shaw in his
summer-house at
Ayot St Lawrence

Dresden, and Frankfurt; and *Candida* was being played in New York. As Shaw always emphasized after he had become successful, it was the Continent and not Britain which first recognized his talents. Nevertheless, the British—or at least a minute section of them—were now for the first time being given the opportunity of seeing his plays at regular intervals. The Stage Society, a semi-amateur group 'started by an energetic Fabian', had done something for him, but its performances were almost private. Not until Shaw was forty-eight were his plays enthusiastically demanded and given full support by a professional management. It was in 1904 that the Vedrenne-Barker management made the experiment of putting on a few matinées of *Candida* at their theatre, the Royal Court in Sloane Square. It was an immediate success; evening performances were given and an association was inaugurated which confirmed, once and for all, Shaw's confidence in himself as a dramatist—a confidence which until then had received almost no support from anybody in the English theatre world.

*Royal Court
Theatre*

Harley Granville-Barker, and indeed the Royal Court enterprise generally, had a high idealism and crusading spirit to match Shaw's own—an almost undergraduate contempt for so-called impossibility, combined with a healthy enjoyment of chatting about their problems. They even communicated their zeal to their friends. Beatrice Webb wrote: 'on Sunday afternoon G.B.S. and Granville-Barker dropped in and spread out before us the difficulties, the

Granville-Barker

John Vedrenne

hopes, the ridiculous aspects of their really arduous efforts to create an intellectual 'drama'. Granville-Barker, himself a playwright and later the author of the *Prefaces to Shakespeare*, was the producer. He was the exact antithesis of Irving: the grand style of acting, the 'star' system, all theatrical hyperbole, offended him; he favoured restraint, attention to meaning rather than effect. Moreover, he was a 'modern' in the plays he chose to produce—*avant-garde* works by such non-commercial writers as Maeterlinck, Galsworthy, Euripides (translated by Gilbert Murray), Shaw, and Barker himself. No ordinary commercial management would touch such certain failures. Granville-Barker made them the talk of London's *avant-garde* circles, the essential topic of conversation for any young man with pretensions to being an artist or intellectual. By giving each play a limited run and repeating it later if it was successful, he and John Vedrenne, an astute business-man who attended to the financial affairs of the management and curbed Granville-Barker's extravagance, managed to keep the theatre solvent, at times even prosperous in a small way, while experienced West End managers muttered predictions of doom and clung to their farces and melodrama.

Rehearsing   Shaw's part in the productions of his plays was not merely passive. He chose the casts, trained them, worked out stage moves using chessmen on a chess-board, contradicted Granville-Barker and generally took a leading part in rehearsals. Considering that he did not scruple to advise such a splendid actress as Ellen Terry 'not to fidget', how to say this and how to move then, it is not surprising that he plunged at his Royal Court players and tore them to pieces—

Harley Granville-Barker, the actor and producer

but without hurting their feelings or reducing them to impotence. His method was to guy the play to them, deliberately over-acting each part, so that they would catch the panache and reproduce it in their own way. And he was no mere theorist: when schooling himself to become a public speaker, he had 'practised the alphabet as a singer practises scales until I was in no danger of saying "Loheeryelentheethisharpointed sword" instead of "Lo here I lend thee thiss sharp pointed sword".'

Candida was a success. Granville-Barker immediately begged Shaw for another play and in due course received *John Bull's Other Island*. This was an even greater success: whether because it dealt with the 'Irish problem' or because its incisive, deflating prose was a relief from the pomposity of Westminster, it attracted Balfour four times and Campbell-Bannerman and Asquith twice each. Better still, Edward VII came to a Command Performance and laughed so much that the chair on which he was sitting collapsed.

John Bull's Other Island had been written 'at the request of Mr William Butler Yeats, as a patriotic contribution to the repertory of the Irish Literary Theatre', then bent on restoring an atmosphere of Celtic mists and vague past glories to

'John Bull's Other Island'

W. B. Yeats, at whose request Shaw
wrote *John Bull's Other Island*,
'as a patriotic contribution to the
repertory of the Irish Literary Theatre'

Ireland. 'Like most people who have asked me to write plays, Mr Yeats got
rather more than he bargained for.' What he got was an unsentimental comedy
about a 'practical' Irishman and a mad priest, with their solutions for the
predicament of Ireland, and a hint of Shaw's ideal Christendom, 'a country
where the State is the Church and the Church the people: three in one and one
in three'.

'Man and Superman', written between 1901 and 1903, entered more deeply into
'philosophy'; it presented existence in terms of the 'Life Force' (a derivation
from Bergson's *élan vital*), driving Woman to pursue Man in order to ensure the
continuance of the species—a theme which, incidentally, recalls Shaw's 'I did
not pursue women: I was pursued by them.' In the published version the play
was followed by *The Revolutionist's Handbook*, supposed to be written by the hero,
a brilliant young man rebelling against the cosy respectability of his elders and
being misunderstood and disliked by them. This contained such gauntlet-
flingings as 'Democracy substituted election by the incompetent many for
appointment by the corrupt few'; 'The vilest abortionist is he who attempts to
mould a child's character'; 'The modern sentimental term for the national

An open-air Salvation Army meeting, of the kind that appears in the first act of *Major Barbara*

minimum of celibacy is Purity'; 'Self-denial is not a virtue: it is only the effect of prudence on rascality.' The play and handbook could not fail to awaken a response in all those who wished to greet the Establishment with thumb to nose. And not only these: 'The smart world,' observed Beatrice Webb, 'is tumbling over one another in the worship of G.B.S., and even we have a sort of reflected glory as his intimate friends. . . . When he is free there is such a crowd of journalists and literary hangers-on around him that one feels it is kinder to spare him one's company.'

Major Barbara, performed in 1905, owed its origins to Shaw's soap-box speeches at the Docks and elsewhere, when he had frequently admired the dramatic skill of the Salvation Army girls conducting meetings near by. He also used the personality of Gilbert Murray as a model for Cusins in the play. It pleased most who saw it, including a contingent of Salvation Army Commissioners, despite the fact that the Army had roundly denounced the theatre as a den of vice, a hive of unspeakable iniquity, a poison as noxious as alcohol. On the other hand, Arthur Balfour, taken to see the première by the faithful Webbs, was 'taken aback by the force, the horrible force of the Salvation Army scene, the unrelieved tragedy of degradation . . . the triumph of the unmoral purpose: the anti-climax of evangelising the Garden City.' And Beatrice Webb herself saw a ruthlessness and detachment in the play which antagonized her.

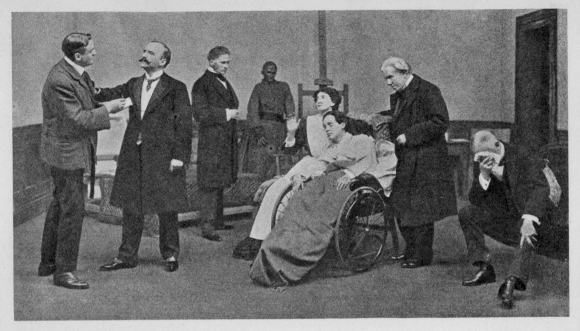

Scene from the first production of *The Doctor's Dilemma*

'*The Doctor's Dilemma*'

Granville-Barker pressed him for more and more plays. Two themes came into his mind. One was the man who has 'certain points of honour, whilst in matters that do not interest him he is careless and unscrupulous'. The other was the rich comedy of medicine and medical practitioners. He had long been a connoisseur of this comedy, sampling cures of every different kind with complete disregard of 'scientific' opinion. His theory was that the specialists were often proved wrong and that their experiments were too dangerous to the patient. Consequently he was always ready to investigate naturopaths, devices like 'Abram's Box' (meant to diagnose illness by examination of a slide of the patient's blood alone), osteopaths, faith healers, and yoga experts. His acquired knowledge of medical eccentricities added to the comedy of *The Doctor's Dilemma*. The character of Louis Dubedat was drawn from Edward Aveling, a man 'morbidly scrupulous as to his religious and political convictions. . . . But he had absolutely no conscience about money and women: he was a shameless seducer and borrower, not to say a thief.'

The play was a success in the Royal Court repertory and spurred Vedrenne and Granville-Barker on to take the Savoy, a West End theatre, where they revived Shaw's *Devil's Disciple*, *Arms and the Man*, and *Caesar and Cleopatra*. But

Scene from the
1906 revival of
*How He Lied
To Her Husband*

their successes were making them over-confident. They took two more West End theatres, for a play by Laurence Housman and Shaw's *Getting Married*, a 'disquisitory play' whose interminable and unrelieved talk did not attract audiences. The management could not stand the strain of these very high over-heads, and it finally collapsed with very small material profits but a vast reputation. During its existence it had put on eleven plays by Shaw: the ones named above, *How He Lied To Her Husband*, *You Never Can Tell*, *Captain Brassbound's Conversion*, *The Philanderer*, *The Man of Destiny*, and *Don Juan in Hell* (the third act of *Man and Superman* performed as a separate play).

Through his successes at the Royal Court Shaw now found himself some-thing of a literary celebrity—still considered a crank and nuisance by the conventional, certainly, but a power among the younger men. Despite his early

Celebrity

Alfred Sutro and Sir Arthur Wing Pinero, two playwrights contemporary with Shaw

dislike of consorting with 'literary men'—'I might have spent my life sitting watching these fellows taking in each other's washing and learning no more of the world than a tic in a typewriter if I had been fool enough'—he now served on the committees of the Stage Society, the Authors' Society and Dramatists' Club, and the Society of Authors. At the meetings of the Dramatists' Club, he came into contact, or rather collision, with the 'old school', the men whom he had belaboured so infuriatingly in the days of the *Saturday Review*—Pinero, Jones, Carton, Grundy, Sutro. They thought him an impudent young devil; Pinero, in particular, always signed his letters to him 'with admiration and detestation'. Nevertheless it was he who advised Ramsay MacDonald, when the latter was Socialist Prime Minister, to confer a knighthood on Pinero. From first to last he insisted on the dignity, and indeed necessity, of the arts. He was even elected to the Council of the Royal Academy of Dramatic Art when a seat became vacant on Sir William Gilbert's death.

As an established dramatist himself, he continually urged other established dramatists to admit younger men to their ranks, partly as an encouragement to them, partly as a way of drawing the younger men's teeth. He also gave the younger men the benefit of his own experience, advising them, in particular,

The Council of the Royal Academy of Dramatic Art (from left to right): Sir George Alexander, Barrie, Pinero, Irene Vanbrugh, Sir Squire Bancroft, C. M. Lawre, Shaw, Sir John Hare, and Sir Johnston Forbes-Robertson

never to under-sell themselves. If, after all, a manager accepted a play from an unknown man, he argued, it was because he could not get anything suitable from an established dramatist: he needed the play and should therefore pay accordingly. In money matters he gradually became more and more ruthless: he would not allow amateur societies to perform his plays for the usual amateur fee but insisted on professional royalties (this sometimes worked out to their advantage, however); insisted on high rates from foreign managements so as not, he said, to act as blackleg towards foreign dramatists; drove close bargains with his publishers, and worried about his income tax.

It was something new for an 'artist' to proclaim openly that he was interested in money. The tradition—a very comfortable one for non-artists—had grown up that artists were above that kind of thing. From the beginning Shaw gloried in haggling over terms (this was another facet of his character that caused the traditionalists to call him 'ungentlemanly'), always representing the other party to the bargain as the winner. 'What is all this about my being extortionate and knowing no middle course in business?' he wrote to Ellen Terry. 'As a matter of fact I have never made a bargain by which a manager has lost. Of course they *say* they lose, because they never study their accounts, and always read

Shaw in his fifties   Mark Twain

Green Room gossip.' As when he put forward some new philosophical, sociological, or artistic theory, he took a tone of sweet reasonableness, always suggesting that he held this view, not out of idealism or sentiment or self-interest, but because it was ultimately to the other man's advantage. 'You say "some folk without selling a play right out, take 5% on the gross receipts." *I* take 10% . . . On the other hand, I dont ask for any advance: so that if the play fails the manager's loss will be much less than mine.'

Mark Twain

All this, however, was taken as part of his eccentric Irish wit—a commodity which found a ready market in the newspapers. Eager reporters snatched interviews with him. One was lucky enough to come upon him by chance when he was awaiting the arrival of Mark Twain (Samuel Clemens) at St Pancras Station. He described the encounter as follows:

'When we saw the slim figure of "G.B.S." strolling on to the platform we were no less surprised than he. . . . "You,"—he beamed characteristically—"you have come to meet Mark Twain, and you have secured the very great advantage of interviewing me."'

Shaw then went about his own business and the gratified reporter betook himself to Mark Twain's side.

'"Do you know," I inquired, "that Mr George Bernard Shaw is upon this platform?" Mark Twain's face lit up. "Is he?" he queried. "I should very much like to see him. I have never met Mr Shaw." Mr Shaw soon came up . . . and the historic introduction took place. It is hard to say which of the two great men looked the more gratified, but Mr Shaw had the advantage from the conversational point of view. "Hardly had I arrived upon this platform," he announced, "than the British Press asked me if you were serious when you wrote 'The Jumping Frog' . . . I can assure you," added Mr Shaw, "that I gave them the correct answer."'

It was at about this time that the Shavian personality began to take shape in the public mind. It was a personality half-clown, half-boor; it amused some, irritated many, and was idolized by a few. He was the man who wore no shirt because he considered it wrong to entwine one's middle in two layers of material and therefore wore 'some head-to-foot under-garment unknown to shirt-makers'. He was the man who, on principle, wore unlined jackets and grey collars. He was the man who, also on principle, addressed his envelopes in the top left-hand corner, claiming that they looked more beautiful that way. He was the man who spelled 'programme' 'program' and 'Shakespeare' 'Shakespear', the man who

The Shavian personality

Harley Granville-Barker
and Charlotte Shaw in 1909

One of the many cartoon portraits of Shaw (by Ruth)

advocated that un-British horror, a combination of the metric and duodecimal systems—'eight, nine, dec, elf, ten, and eighteen, nineteen, decteen, elfteen, twenty, and so forth'. He was the man who took a dip in the swimming-pool of the Royal Automobile Club every morning before breakfast throughout the year. He was the man with such a passion for machines that he once nearly bought a cash register merely because he was fascinated by it, and such an inability to use them that he was constantly having accidents—once riding into a Great Western Railway van outside the National Gallery, on another occasion shooting off a motor-bicycle outside his own front door, in later life involving his wife in a serious motor accident. He was the man who called marriage a form of legalized prostitution and schoolmasters slave-drivers. He was the vegetarian, the anti-vivisectionist, the militant non-smoker.

It was he who spurned sentimentality of all kinds, lived on his mother until he was married and then neglected her company more or less completely until her death. (He did, however, send her constant money contributions, a fact he never publicized, as being out of tune with the character he had created for himself.) It was he who, after attacking Irving throughout his lifetime, dealt him an unmerciful blow after his death when he could not answer back. Actually this last episode was not quite so brutal as it was painted in the Press. After Irving's death the *Neue Freie Presse* of Vienna asked Shaw to write them an

Shaw as a car-driver

obituary and he sent them an 'objective' critical article containing the sentences: 'The truth is, Irving was interested in nothing but himself and the self in which he was interested was an imaginary self in an imaginary world. He lived in a dream.' The relative part of this was translated into German as *'nur eine imaginäre Person in einer imaginären Pose'* and re-translated into English by the Press, which leaped upon it, as 'He was a narrow-minded egoist, devoid of culture, and living on the dream of his own greatness.' The original was hurtful enough at a moment when the grief at Irving's death was still raw; the re-translation was beyond even a Shavian joke. Who could blame Laurence Irving when he wrote to Shaw that 'my kindred, with the exception of my wife and myself, tell me you are a monstrous Yahoo for whom nothing but excommunication is fitting'? Ellen Terry, who had soothed all Shaw's wounds in the early days of his professional life, who had listened so sympathetically to all his idealism and difficulties, and who had loved Irving dearly, was bitterly hurt. 'You never wrote the words they say you wrote, except when Henry was well, was at work and *fighting*. Then it was all right enough—fair. You never said it I'm sure when all his friends were sore and smarting. *You* don't add hyssop to the wounds. That would be *unfair*.' Nevertheless it was part of the fantastically inhuman character that Shaw was deliberately building up for himself. He refused to go

Death of Irving

Herbert Samuel was Chairman of the
Parliamentary Commission on stage
censorship to which Shaw
gave evidence

Censorship

to Irving's funeral in Westminster Abbey, on the grounds 'that Literature has no place at Irving's graveside'.

Nobody was greatly disconcerted when he launched an attack on the system of play-censorship then in operation. His amorality was too generally suspected. It was more surprising that he should be associated in this matter with the beneficent Herbert (now Lord) Samuel, the whimsical Barrie, the respectable Galsworthy, the merry Catholic Chesterton, William Archer, Israel Zangwill, Arthur Pinero, and others. Shaw had written a short play called *The Shewing-Up of Blanco Posnet* which was banned by the Lord Chamberlain mainly because Blanco says of God: 'He's a sly one. He's a mean one. He lies low for you. He plays cat and mouse with you. . . . He lets you run loose until you think you are shut of him; and then, when you least expect it, he's got you.' It was performed, however, at the Abbey Theatre, Dublin, over which the Lord Chamberlain had no jurisdiction, but its banning, together with a growing feeling of antagonism towards the whole machinery of stage-censorship, led to

Sir James Barrie
who lived opposite the
Shaws in London

the appointment by the Government of a Joint Committee of the House of Lords and the House of Commons on Stage Plays (Censorship). Herbert Samuel was the Chairman and the resultant Blue Book contained statements by the above-mentioned writers. Shaw put forth all his talent for argument against a system which could, as he said, strip a playwright of both his livelihood and his good name and allow him no legal opportunity of taking redress. The committee managed to eradicate a good many anomalies and injustices although stage-censorship remains a problem to this day.

James Barrie, one of the censorship-attackers, lived opposite the Shaws' *Barrie* London home. He and the Shaws did not meet frequently; perhaps he was repelled by a friend's remark that he could always put forward as his claim to immortality that he lived opposite George Bernard Shaw. However, he was one of the few who managed to deflate him by his own methods. Once, at a dinner, the little Scot rose to his feet and said: 'When I first came to London, I was overawed by a remarkable young man who was then taking it by storm. He

Keir Hardie, the first Labour Member of Parliament, with the Shaws

knew about everything: music, drama, Socialism, philosophy.' Shaw, who was present, smiled modestly down at his dinner-plate. 'I wonder,' said Barrie speculatively, 'what has become of that young man now.'

Shaw resolved to make him an innocent catspaw in his latest publicity move. When *Fanny's First Play* was produced in 1911, he told everyone concerned to suggest that it was by his sprightly neighbour. Nobody was taken in for long, but the initial mystery attracted attention and large enough audiences for the play to be called a fair success (it ran for over six hundred performances). But this was nothing compared with the success which was to follow in the succeeding year—the Shavian best-seller, the play which suddenly jerked Shaw into the consciousness of the general public.

'Androcles and the Lion' However, before this was staged London audiences were nonplussed by *Androcles and the Lion*, a presentation of early Christianity, with its martyrdoms and fervour, in terms of what Shaw called 'a pantomime'; he imagined it would appeal to children. The pith of the play was in the Preface; here Shaw

Statue of Joan of Arc at
Orleans which Shaw saw
and remarked on during
a visit to France in 1911

stated his view of Christianity. He took a fresh look at the figure of Christ,
uninfluenced by the accumulated bulk of theology, custom, and racial and
religious prejudice and drew a parallel between Christ's Christianity and true,
theoretical Communism, the Communism in which he himself believed. Once
and for all he disposed of all forms of orthodoxy: 'Thus it is not disbelief that is
dangerous to society: it is belief.' But he showed himself so sympathetic to
Christ as he appears in the Gospels rather than in Church practice that
many people began to revise their opinion that Shaw was nothing but a
scoffer.

After a couple of months, however, the novelty of religious pantomime wore
off. By the time *Androcles* was taking only £850 a week in a theatre that cost
£1000 Shaw decided that he needed a holiday and went off to France. He
visited several towns, including Moulins Allier, Valence, and Rouen, but it was
Orleans that made the deepest impression on him. He found it permeated
through and through with the story of Joan of Arc.

'I shall do a Joan play some day [he wrote]. I should have God about to damn the English for their share in her betrayal and Joan producing an end of burnt stick in arrest of Judgment. "What's that? Is it one of the faggots?" says God. "No," says Joan, "it's what is left of two sticks a common English soldier tied together and gave me as I went to the stake".'

Some twenty years later he wrote the play.

Androcles and the Lion was taken off and for a while there was a lull: a few Shavian plays were revived. And then, suddenly, London was delighted, startled, and vastly diverted by a new comedy: *Pygmalion*.

On 8 September 1897 Shaw had written to Ellen Terry of Forbes-Robertson and Mrs Patrick Campbell: 'I would teach that rapscallionly flower girl of his something. *Caesar and Cleopatra* has been driven clean out of my head by a play I want to write for them in which he shall be a west end gentleman and she an east end dona in an apron and three orange and red ostrich feathers.'

The idea lingered in his mind for fifteen years until one day the actor-manager George Alexander asked him for a play. He remembered the Cockney flower-girl, the ostrich feathers, and the general theme, and, already fascinated by Mrs Patrick Campbell's beauty and charm, wrote *Pygmalion* specially for her. The only question was whether Mrs Pat, known for her pride and vagaries, would accept the part of 'Liza Doolittle, a flower girl, using awful language and wearing an apron and three ostrich feathers, and having her hat put in the oven to slay the creepy-crawlies, and being taken off the stage to be washed.' For some time he lacked the courage to say to her, 'Here is a part that fits you down to the ground, in which your personality can have full play.' At last he hit on the device of asking a friend to let him read it to her, contriving that Mrs Pat should be there at the same time. The famous actress came, heard, and was fascinated. 'She saw through it like a shot. "You beast, you wrote this for me, every line of it: I can hear you mimicking my voice in it, etc. etc." And she rose to the occasion, quite fine and dignified for a necessary moment, and said unaffectedly she was flattered.'

However, for once Shaw had met his match. Stella, as Mrs Patrick Campbell was known to her friends, was as self-willed as he, as single-minded where business was concerned, and almost as intelligent. Unfortunately she did not occupy such a strong position: if she antagonized actors or managers they could usually find a substitute for her, whereas there were no other dramatists who could replace Shaw. She began by insisting on going into management for *Pygmalion*, instead of letting some other manager take the profits. Then she quarrelled about who was to be the leading man, rejecting all Shaw's suggestions as impossible and putting forward even more impossible suggestions herself.

Mrs Patrick Campbell (as Mrs Ebbsmith in *The Notorious Mrs Ebbsmith*)

Herbert Beerbohm Tree, the first Professor Higgins

Shaw at Ayot St Lawrence

After having blackened the character of Robert Loraine (one of Shaw's suggestions) she received a shock when Shaw repeated all she had said to Loraine. He returned her opinion with interest, Shaw carried all his insults back to Stella and 'finally they had to assure one another of their undying esteem and admiration, which was what I wanted'. However, Loraine had to fulfil various commitments in America and so *Pygmalion* was still without a leading man. In disgust, Shaw went off to Europe with Charlotte and her sister, left them at Kissingen undergoing a cure—'mud baths and the like'—and, after another of his motoring mishaps, ended, gloomily, in Nancy.

Beerbohm Tree
The next candidate for Professor Higgins was Sir Herbert Tree, the manager of His Majesty's Theatre. After various disagreements, misunderstandings, and tantrums from all parties, the affair was settled: Tree would play Higgins, Stella Eliza Doolittle, and the play would be put on at His Majesty's

Tree was a difficult man to deal with in rehearsal. He remained, throughout a long and successful professional career, essentially an amateur, with an amateur's

Mrs Patrick Campbell as Eliza Doolittle

casualness about breaking up rehearsals if a friend called to see him, inviting any acquaintances to come along and witness rehearsals, invading the territory of some specialists, such as designers and stage-managers, and leaving others completely without guidance, until Shaw was driven to despair. Shaw thought him a muddler; he thought Shaw excessively interfering. 'I seem to have heard or read somewhere,' he said once, in mild reproach, 'that plays have actually been produced, and performances given, in this theatre, under its present management, before you came. According to you that couldn't have happened. How do you account for it?'

Nevertheless, despite all the trials of rehearsal, Sir Herbert's over-sanguine temperament, Stella's occasional fits of temperament, and Shaw's unwelcome advice on every point of acting, production, casting, and stage-management, *Pygmalion* opened on the night for which it was announced and was received with a delight which has never diminished whenever it has been revived, in the theatre, as a film, or as the libretto of a musical.

Shaw's attitude towards the sinking of the *Titanic* (shown here on her trials) caused him to become unpopular in certain quarters

The Titanic

Shaw became the fashion. No longer the idol of a small côterie only, he suddenly seemed to attract publicity in whatever he touched. Even before the success of *Pygmalion* the general public had begun to expect to see some pronouncement from him on any event which filled the headlines. In 1912, for instance, when the *Titanic*, the largest and most splendid ocean liner then afloat, had sunk after striking an iceberg and 1,490 lives had been lost, he had written to the *Daily News* scoffing at the 'sentimental idiots with a break in the voice' who praised the gallantry of the sailors and passengers. On the contrary, he said, the whole accident had been brought about by gross mismanagement on the part of the captain, officers, and crew alike; lifeboats had hastened to safety leaving others stranded, men had snatched at places before women could reach them, the cries of those struggling in the water had been disregarded. It may have been true, though later reports only half-confirmed his analysis, but it was not consoling to the bereaved relatives of the drowned crew and passengers. Sir Arthur Conan Doyle sprang furiously to their defence, called him a sadist,

Cartoon depicting a Fabian
debate between Shaw and Belloc

pointed out several errors in his facts and, naturally, attracted all the sympathy
to himself. Shaw remained unrepentant: he wanted to influence the future
conduct of such liners, not weep over the past.

After *Pygmalion*, Shaw's name or face seemed hardly ever to be out of the
newspapers. It might be a report of a public debate with G. K. Chesterton and
Hilaire Belloc, two great friends whom he nevertheless attacked constantly for
their excessive devotion to Catholicism and a political doctrine which struck
him as jejune. These debates attracted huge audiences. The personalities of the
speakers were delightful in themselves—Shaw, tall, flamboyant, Irish and
devil-may-care; Chesterton enormously fat, enormously good-humoured; Belloc,
the man who opened one debate by announcing to the audience, '*You* are about
to listen, *I* am about to sneer.' Chesterton was very fond of Shaw, both as a
sparring partner and as a man. He saw through the pose of complete flippancy;

The Chesterbelloc

85

Still from a film burlesque in which Barrie persuaded Shaw to take part (left to right: Lord Howard de Walden, William Archer, Barrie, Chesterton, and Shaw)

on the contrary the only constraint between them arose out of Shaw's essential seriousness, his temperamental inability to let his hair down with complete abandon. At one party, for instance, the company boiled an egg in Sir Herbert Tree's hat, it being the shiniest and smartest; Chesterton fought a duel with another equally intoxicated guest; Shaw became more and more bored and left the scene. However, on another occasion he was persuaded by Barrie to take part in an irresponsible frolic—a silent burlesque film of a Western, in which Chesterton, Belloc, and Shaw played cowboys and at one point Shaw had to roll down a hill in a barrel. This was done for the benefit of the Red Cross.

But such frivolous amusements were rare. In general his frivolity was reserved for the enhancement, and hence propagation, of serious topics—serious, at least, to Shaw.

Unlike any other literary man before or after him, he claimed to speak with authority—the authority of the sensible non-specialist—on every subject. It was not only drama, music, art, Socialism, and philosophy which interested him. He had, and broadcast, his own views on science, to the ridicule of his scientist friends, H. G. Wells, J. S. Haldane, and others. The idea of vivisection outraged him; he deluged the Press with accusations that the scientists practising

Charlotte in the first year of her marriage

it were 'scoundrels'. Again he took the 'sensible' line: they perpetrated horrible tortures, he said, to prove what could be proved much more easily and quickly by simple observation. Wells pointed out that 'the vast mass of experiments and observations recorded required as a primary condition that the animals should be altogether calm and comfortable'. He might just as well have held his breath. When Shaw had once taken up an attitude he rarely dropped it.

The same was true of his later advocacy of a reformed alphabet of forty-four letters, each representing one sound in the English language. His main argument in favour of this idea was that it would save time and money: 'The time saved by phonetic will come out round about twenty per cent. . . . Now there are 525,000 minutes in a year, consequently the saving of twenty per cent per minute means a labour saving of two months' working days per scribe every year.' It was pointed out to him that the saving in time would not be by any means so considerable as he imagined, since few people either read or write by reference to individual letters, but grasp the word as a whole; also that all printing presses, existing books, and typewriters would have to be changed simultaneously or else that children would have to learn both spelling-systems. But he always found his own reasoning more convincing than others'.

Reformed alphabet

Shaw swimming in the South of France

Press photographers followed the Shaws everywhere they went, taking pictures of Shaw bathing, walking, sunning himself, in every posture. And besides these unrehearsed encounters, he was portrayed again and again by painters, sculptors, and draughtsmen. As Wells said, in exasperation: 'His extraordinary industry in sitting to painters, photographers and sculptors will fill the museums of the future with entire galleries of his portraits, medals, statues and busts.' Rodin was the first to make a bust of him. It was Charlotte who insisted on her husband's being portrayed by the great French artist. After the sittings were over, Rodin was asked how Shaw spoke French. 'Mr Shaw does not speak French well,' he replied, 'but he expresses himself with such violence that he imposes himself.' Rodin was followed by Paul Troubetzkoy, Davidson, Sigmund Strobl, and Epstein in sculpture, Augustus John, William Rothenstein, John Collier, and many others in two-dimensional art.

The Shavian personality became a favourite standby for journalists when other news was in short supply. Interesting items of information were singled

Shaw and Gene Tunney,
the American heavyweight boxer,
one of his friends

out: his friendship with Gene Tunney, the boxer, for instance; his habit of doing singing-practice at the piano every night as a health measure (he maintained that it was good for the lungs); his fondness for walking, his learning to dance the tango when in his sixties. Best of all he could usually be relied on for some monumentally conceited statement which would have half their readers snorting in disgust and the other half chuckling with appreciation. Those who admired Shaw found his honest appreciation of his own worth as refreshing a relief from the usual cant as his directness towards all other subjects. As he himself wrote:

'When an actress writes her memoirs, she impresses on you in every chapter how sorely it tries her feelings to exhibit her person to the public gaze; but she does not forget to decorate the book with a dozen portraits of herself. I really

Shaw in the Parthenon with a group of Greek newspapermen who had come to interview him

cannot respond to this demand for mock modesty. I am ashamed neither of my work nor of the way it is done. I like explaining its merits to the huge majority who dont know good work from bad.'

Travels   Charlotte forced him to travel a good deal, mostly under protest: 'I am at least quit of Athens with its stupid classic Acropolis and smashed pillars.' 'This [the Mediterranean] is a brute of a place, morally hideous, physically only pretty-pretty. . . . I was born to bite the north wind, not to soak in this lukewarm Reckitt's blue purlieu of gamblers.' He called Milan Cathedral a vulgarly expensive wedding-cake and St Mark's a railway terminus which had been put to the wrong use. On the other hand he was enthralled by Beauvais Cathedral: 'I had my breath taken away literally and physically when I first stepped into the giant choir which is all that remains of the Cathedral at Beauvais.'

Anatole France   August Strindberg, who entertained Shaw in Stockholm

In the Sistine Chapel in Rome he accidentally met Anatole France, as much of a legend, though a less controversial one, in his own country, as Shaw was in England. When France asked him who he was Shaw merely replied: 'Like yourself, a man of genius.' To which the Frenchman deflatingly muttered: 'Ah well; a whore has the right to call herself a pleasure merchant.' In Stockholm Shaw called on Strindberg and peppered him with energetic advice as to who should translate his works into English. There was little sympathy between the two men; Shaw, with his unlimited activity and forthrightness, made Strindberg feel tired and neurotic almost before the conversation had begun.

Despite all these travels, Shaw remained a poor linguist until the end of his life, a fact which did not deter him from translating a play by his own German translator, Siegfried Trebitsch, into English. In the process it changed from a tragedy into a Shavian comedy; Shaw remained more or less unmoved when Trebitsch pointed this out to him.

But in the midst of all this much-publicized activity, Shaw was undergoing an experience almost completely novel for him. Ever since the episode of Mrs Jenny Patterson he had been used to the worship and pursuit of women

Mrs Patrick Campbell and George Alexander in Pinero's *The Second Mrs Tanqueray*

admirers. 'Whenever I have been left alone with a woman,' he complained, 'she has invariably thrown her arms round me and declared she adored me.' Now, almost for the first time in his life, in his late middle age, he himself became entirely besotted with a woman who was herself the idol of most men who came into contact with her.

'I went calmly to her house to discuss business with her, as hard as nails, [he wrote to Ellen Terry] and, as I am a living man, fell head over ears in love with her in thirty seconds. And it lasted more than thirty hours. I made no struggle: I went head over ears and dreamed and dreamed and walked on air for all that afternoon and the next day as if my next birthday were my twentieth.'

Mrs Pat   It was Mrs Patrick Campbell who wrought the miracle of making Shaw want, for once, to throw off the artificial outer crust of personality which he had so carefully built up round himself. 'I am trying hard not to act. There are such wonderful sorts of relations, such quaint comforts and happiness and close‚ togethernesses . . .' But Stella was a highly intelligent woman, and a woman of great perception. From the first she saw that her fervent admirer was imprisoned in his own legend, the legend of 'Joey the clown' with his 'cap‚and‚bells and bladder‚whacking', combined with the legends of Shaw the reformer, Shaw the earnest of purpose. After decades of senti-ment-disparagement, it was rather too late for him to succumb to emotion without reservations, although for a short space he was really moved by love.

He was present when Stella had a splinter removed from under her thumbnail and the pain that her pain caused him opened his eyes to all that had become artificial and remote in his attitude towards other people.

'My dearest love: I think all that was good for my soul, because it tore everything that was selfish and imaginary right out of me, and made you a real fellow-creature in real pain (O Lord! my fibres all twist and my heart and bowels torment me when I think of it); and the more real you become the more I discover that I have a real real kind-ness for you, and that I am not a mere connoisseur in beauty or a sensualist or a philanderer, but a—but a—a—a—I dont know what, but something that has deep roots in it that you pluck at. Only, why should you have to be hurt to cure me of selfishness and little fits of acting?'

For months he plied her with letters full of the most ardent emotion, while accom-panying his wife and sister-in-law round Europe or rehearsing plays in London. Her name was so constantly on his lips that Sidney Webb declared that it was a clear case of sexual senility. He went to a Fabian Summer School at Sedbergh to take his mind off her—and spent most of his time walking over the fells talking of her to Rebecca West, a brilliant young journalist. He worried about her health, her finances, her career. He revelled in dreams, but all the while knew that they were dreams and did not belong to 'real' life.

Shaw leaving His Majesty's Theatre after the production of *Pygmalion*

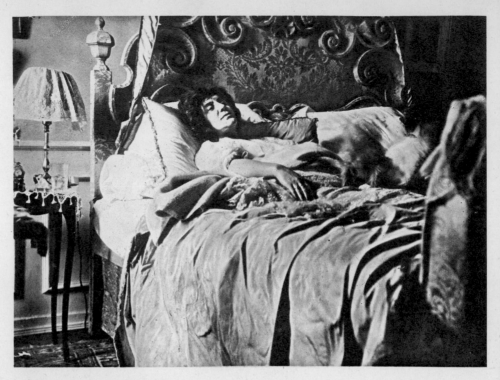

Mrs Patrick Campbell in bed

For, of course, Charlotte was the 'real' woman; and Charlotte was bitterly jealous of what she learned or suspected of the affair. 'I am all torn to bits: you dont know what it is to me to be forced to act artificially when everything has been freshly stirred in me. . . . But the worst of it is that all our conversation was overheard: and the effect was dreadful: it hurts me miserably to see anyone suffer like that.'

Gradually 'reality' asserted itself more and more and resumed its old ascendancy over the Shavian personality. Even at the height of the fury, he had always considered Charlotte's feelings. Once, at the house in Kensington Square, Stella teasingly tried to make him late for an appointment with his wife: he protested, she attempted to hold him back by force and a servant came into the room just as they fell on to the floor in a dusty scuffle. (Shaw used this whole incident, exactly as it occurred, in *The Apple Cart*.)

It was not long before the last, and almost the first, passion had ended and Mrs Patrick Campbell reverted to her old identity as a beautiful but trying actress whose fits of temperament made her difficult to work with—yet another candidate

Mrs Patrick Campbell's
house in Kensington Square

for Shavian flattery and verbal flirtation. Shaw had never fully appreciated her acute intellect; he always divided people into those whose words he listened to and those whose charms he admired. Nevertheless, from her unique position as one who had really probed the depths of Shaw's deliberate self-alienation from people at his own level, she had laid her finger on what may be called a failing in some of his plays—at least where he attempted to deal with the feeling, rather than the thinking, side of human nature: 'You beget your dramatis personae like a God—but as you went along you lost respect for their bones . . . and it gives a boneless locomotor-ataxy effect and the people become mere mouthpieces of the general scheme—without flesh and blood—I feel *disorder* where you would probably feel "there I was inspired."'

After the end of the affair her fortunes declined. She was becoming old; despite her still great beauty and talent, she found it more and more difficult to get work in the theatre, and what little money she earned was mortgaged in

Scene from the first production of *John Bull's Other Island*

advance, for she was heavily in debt. So, many years later, she decided to publish her autobiography, including letters from her past admirers—Shaw, Barrie, and many others. By this time the fever which had once burned in Shaw had been completely extinguished: he could not even remember what it had felt like and re-read his letters with embarrassment. He was now completely and irrevocably ensconced in his position as world pontiff, viewing the activities of the rest of this planet from some loftier perch. He gave a curt refusal, pleading the *convenances*: 'Any capable and experienced woman of the world will tell you without a moment's hesitation, and with considerable surprise at your having any doubt on the subject, that their publication is utterly impossible.' In his mind the whole affair had become merely a sordid escape from the normalities of life, to be acknowledged as such by all parties and buried in oblivion: 'Do you ever read breach-of-promise cases? Or divorce cases? Do you ever shudder at the way in which the letters are served up cold to the ridicule or the pruriency or the simple scandalous curiosity of [the public]?'

He ended by asking querulously what she would say if he proposed to publish her letters. The answer came back with all the directness of a personality which

Shaw's mother in old age

was not obliged to maintain itself but existed of its own right. 'Any letters of mine you may publish, if you will correct the grammar and see to the punctuation.' The wrangle over the subject continued at intervals for some years; it was never fully resolved, nor the letters published, in Mrs Patrick Campbell's lifetime. So ended Shaw's one passion.

In 1913, while all this was going on, Shaw's mother died. Shaw, attending the cremation, was entranced at the sight of the garnet-coloured flames leaping up around the coffin, and amused when officials delicately sorted out the remains of the corpse from the debris of the burned coffin. He could feel, he said, his mother smiling down at the sight over his shoulder, and so hilarious was he that Granville-Barker, who had gone to the funeral with him, exclaimed in shocked amazement: 'Shaw, you certainly are a merry soul.'

His mother's death

But even this qualified merriment was abruptly terminated in the following four years. To the public at large Shaw was Joey the Clown—a crank, a comic,

Crowds cheering when War was declared in 1914

a man who would always hold the unconventional view on principle. That was all right, amusing enough, when it concerned only harmless things like philosophy, the arts, and long-term sociology; but when it came to serious matters, such as the War, it was dangerous, hateful, unbearable. As early as 1912 and 1913 he had started to campaign for a pact between Britain, France, and the United States to which all grievances would be referred. In 1914, at the height of the excitement, when the country was so jingoistically enthusiastic that irate letters were written to the Press denouncing dachshund-owners as traitors, he published *Commonsense About the War*, in which he attacked Britain's policies, in particular Sir Edward Grey's dithering, and appeared to support the Sinn Feiners in Ireland.

The Great War

The whole country seemed to rise against him. Newspapers screamed that the public should boycott his plays; Asquith, who had so much enjoyed *John Bull's Other Island*, declared that he ought to be shot; old friends cut him. When, in addition, he protested against the national melodrama over the sinking of the *Lusitania*—'"Killing saloon passengers! What next!" was the essence of the

The Flanders Front in the 1914–18 War

whole agitation'—while thousands of men were being uselessly killed at the Front through governmental mismanagement, the screams and shouting rose to an even higher pitch. The Dramatists' Club formally expelled him; a fellow-member of the Society of Authors marched out of a committee-meeting where he was present, shouting, 'I will not sit in the room with Mr Bernard Shaw'; another writer demanded that he be tarred and feathered. Even personal friends attacked him: Arnold Bennett called his remarks inopportune, Sutro ill-timed, Galsworthy tasteless, Conrad undignified. His mail was swelled by thousands of letters calling him everything from a traitor to a congenital idiot; he had only to step outside his front door to be met with some fresh insult. Yet he faced this almost universal onslaught with courage and even jauntiness: 'I appeared on the London platform at the end of October and lectured twice on the war. Riots were expected; but the result was three hundred people turned away and only two questions, both about Jesus Christ. Similar results next time.' And the Belgians still thought sufficiently well of his reputation to invite him, along with other eminent authors, to contribute to King Albert's Gift-Book in aid of

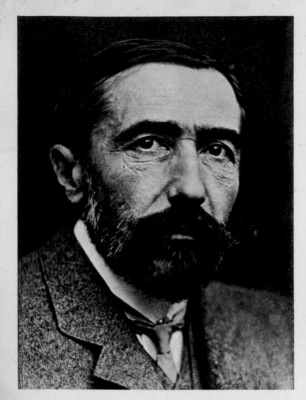

Joseph Conrad and Arnold Bennett both attacked Shaw for his attitude towards the First World War

funds for Belgian war-victims. He also provided a story called *The Emperor and the Little Girl* for a Belgian war-charity.

When he also came out in support of Roger Casement, the Irishman being tried for treason at that time, his stock sank to its lowest depths. Yet he wrote: 'While the war lasts it will never be safe to have a play of mine running; for if I have another piece of my mind to give to this silly nation, nothing will stop me.'

The post-war world

The war destroyed more than merely Shaw's popularity and so many hundreds of thousands of soldiers' lives. For years after it the older generation mourned the lost pre-1914 era almost as though it were a separate life, a world apart. After 1918 almost all the dignities remaining from the long Victorian Age, many of them traditional targets for Shavian wit and abuse—the large staffs of servants, the elaborate respect for the Season, the women's full-length, heavily corseted dresses and plume-ridden hats—were found to have died the quiet death of expediency. In their place were disillusionment, jazz, short skirts, flat chests, and flappers.

Sylvia Pankhurst
addressing a crowd
that had gathered
round the Suffragettes'
premises

Women aged thirty and over now had the vote after a long and tiring struggle
for it, in which the Shaws had taken a modest part. Charlotte, waved on by her
husband, had marched in at least one procession; and Shaw had given a
lecture for Sylvia Pankhurst's '"Mother's Arms"—not Mrs Pankhurst's but a
public house which S. has converted into a school for mothers.' He also
supported Mrs Bright and the Suffragettes by refusing to enter his wife's income
on a joint tax-return, thereby calling down on his head accusations that even
he, the Arch-Socialist, evaded taxation when it was applied to his own property.
One country, Russia, was now actually under Socialist control after the two
revolutions of 1917.

In short, many of the more material moons he had bayed for fell into his lap;
and the changing mood of society was making it increasingly difficult to laugh
at. In any case London did not have the benefit of much Shavian laughter
during the War. It was becoming more and more difficult for managements to
take risks with controversial plays: 'Rents went up to an unprecedented figure,'
Shaw observed. 'At the same time prices doubled everywhere except at the
theatre pay-boxes, and raised the expenses of management to such a degree that
unless the houses were quite full every night, profit was impossible. Even bare
solvency could not be attained without a very wide popularity.'

One of the Suffragette demonstrations

So he contented himself with a few trifles—*The Inca of Perusalem*, *Annajanska*, *O'Flaherty, V.C.*, and *Augustus Does His Bit*, two topical war-pieces; and *The Great Catherine*, written for Gertrude Kingston, one of those plays where, Shaw admitted with characteristic and un-authorlike honesty, 'the author has to use his skill as the actors' tailor, fitting them with parts written to display the virtuosity of the performer rather than to solve the problems of life, characters or history'. But he had been working on *Heartbreak House* and this was finished in 1919 and performed in New York in the following year.

'Heartbreak House'

In a curious way, *Heartbreak House* tastes of the disillusionment then flavouring everything. Shaw was not particularly representative of the ages he lived through, but he, like his contemporaries, was overtaken by a feeling of nothingness and despair. Before 1914 his spirits had never flagged as he fought for reform in politics, art, human conduct generally; there was always a hope, however small, of success. But the War made it brutally plain that that hope was unfounded. It may have been true that there were 'thinking' households in

Scene from the first London production of *Heartbreak House*

plenty, that 'without at least a few plays by myself and Mr Granville Barker, and a few stories by Mr H. G. Wells, Mr Arnold Bennett, and Mr John Galsworthy, the house [of the cultured man] would have been out of the movement', but as far as the conduct of government and the temper of the nation were concerned, such households might just as well not have existed. In *Heartbreak House* he showed the representatives of the opposite views, Hushabye, Mangan, and Utterword, in power, while Captain Shotover, the only one who cares about the power of the mind, is old, defeated, and rooted in the past.

This gloom was not appreciated by London audiences (although the play remained in the regular repertory at Vienna and did quite satisfactory business in New York) and Shaw was faced by yet another failure, one which rankled more than any before. He was, after all, sixty-four and he could not know that he had almost another thirty years ahead of him. Life is short; what had he achieved? If only life could be extended to a more reasonable length, so that men could come to full maturity and the race be thoroughly reinvigorated.

Scene from the first production in America of *Back to Methuselah*

'Back to Methuselah'

Whether or not Shaw ever really thought along these lines, his next play was to be on that theme; this was *Back to Methuselah*, in reality a cycle of five plays taking place in 4004 B.C., A.D. 1920, A.D. 2170, A.D. 3000, and A.D. 31,920. The Lord Chancellor refused to license it as a single work and charged him the reading fee for five plays. Its length is one of its most striking characteristics; the other is the emphasis it lays on continuation: this life as we know it is not enough; there must be something more.

Even Shaw had no illusions as to its commercial possibilities; when the Theatre Guild of New York asked permission to produce it he wrote: 'A contract is unnecessary. It isnt likely that any other lunatics will want to produce it,' and his reply to Barry Jackson's similar request was, quite simply, 'Is your family provided for?' In fact, the whole story of the play's production in America is an indication of Shaw's huge cultural prestige. Lawrence Langner, a staunch culture-supporter and one of the founders of the Theatre Guild of New York, insisted on putting the play on and after a run of nine weeks it proved to have lost some 20,000 dollars. When Shaw apologized for this, Langner actually attempted to comfort him, saying that the loss was amply offset by the respect the Guild had won in attempting such an artistic masterpiece.

Sir Sydney Cockerell,
through whom
Shaw came to know both the
Abbess of Stanbrook and, later,
T. E. Lawrence

The play's philosophical thesis—the rejection of Darwinism or pre-destination in favour of Lamarckinism or free will—was more important to Shaw than its potentialities as a money-maker. His mystical side was coming more and more to dominate his debunking side.

On 24 April 1924 he began a curious acquaintance which, only a few years before, would have seemed entirely out of character. An old associate of his, Sir Sydney Cockerell, had for long been a friend and admirer of the Abbess of Stanbrook in Worcestershire, an enclosed nun who had, as Shaw said, an unenclosed mind. A student of liturgical and medieval learning and a woman of great human understanding, the Lady Abbess was nevertheless firmly convinced of the essential and unalterable rightness of Catholic Christianity and the error of all other religions. Shaw believed that the prophets did not cease with the last page of the Bible, that saintliness and divine revelation could be found outside the Church—any church—and that Christ's teaching was inestimably valuable because it corresponded with the teaching of any truly

*The Abbess of
Stanbrook*

The Abbess of Stanbrook

humanitarian heart, not the other way about. Opinions are not necessarily a barrier between men, but where the opinions dominate the whole character, it is surely rare for a strong communion of the spirit to emerge. Yet between Shaw and the Abbess such a communion existed, despite her distaste and forthright condemnation of much that he wrote. Again and again he turned his back on the turmoil of the theatre and politics, and made his way through the quiet grounds of the Abbey to the grille in the parlour behind which sat his tranquil but unyielding friend. He admired her charm, intellect, sense of humour, and indifference to things of the body—an indifference which, for different reasons, he had always felt and advocated himself; she, in her turn, praised his 'absolute sincerity and simplicity'. With grateful humility, he begged the Abbess and her nuns to remember him in their prayers:

Stanbrook Abbey

'As I drove back here it was a magically lovely evening, or seemed so to me.
I felt ever so much the better for your blessing. There are some people who,
like Judas Iscariot, have to be damned as a matter of heavenly business; . . . but
if I try to sneak into paradise behind you they will be too glad to see you to
notice me.'

Dame Laurentia's attention had been drawn to the existence of this
'blasphemer' by the success of *St Joan*. Sir Sydney Cockerell had sent her a copy *'St Joan'*
and she had found it 'a wonderful play, reaching in its simplicity (which must
have cost much labour) a high degree of art'. She was not alone in this view;
with the production of *St Joan* in London and New York, Shaw acquired the
status of a sage, and all his pronouncements were received as oracles. The theme
itself had been suggested to him almost fortuitously. Joan of Arc had just been
canonized when, looking about him for a subject for a new play, he asked
Charlotte if she had any ideas. 'Why not Joan of Arc?' she suggested. The
idea, which had passed through his mind twenty years earlier, now gripped

Sybil Thorndike as St Joan in the first production of the play

The New York St Joan

him; here was the 'first Protestant', a woman of immense power and drive, a woman answering, as it were, the purposes of a Super-Life Force, allowing herself no self-indulgences but the joys of spirituality—an ascetic, but an ascetic without sentimentality. His version of her was not strictly historical; but it rose at times to the heights of poetry and captured the imaginations of Catholics and Protestants alike. At last, the public seemed to say, he has chosen to be serious on a subject worth being serious about—not crank philosophies, not unwanted reforms, not unbelievable scientific doctrines, but 'real' religion.

Suddenly, and almost for the first time, he was taken seriously. His seventieth birthday was greeted by hundred of telegrams, presents, congratulations from the German Foreign Secretary, and a dinner given him by friends in the Labour Party who presented him with a silver ink-stand inscribed 'Will he ever die? Not bloody likely.' He had always had an aversion to birthdays and other

A public debate between Shaw, Hilaire Belloc, and G. K. Chesterton

automatic and generally unjustified celebrations. 'I have long ceased to celebrate my own birthday,' he declared in the nineties; 'and I do not see why I should celebrate Shakespear's.'

Nobel Prize

However, his dislike of such things could not stop countries, municipalities, and organizations showering him with honours on the smallest opportunity. The Nobel Prize was awarded to him in 1925. He donated the prize money to the Anglo-Swedish Literary Alliance for the promotion of 'intercourse and understanding in literature and art between Sweden and the British Isles'. When the Labour Party came into power in 1924, Ramsay MacDonald offered him a knighthood or peerage, but he refused, saying that his works had given him all the distinction he required. Galsworthy persuaded him to join the P.E.N. Club, an international association of writers. He was invited to be a pall-bearer at Thomas Hardy's funeral in Westminster Abbey. After remarking that 'I havent any proper clothes,' he nevertheless added his shoulder to those of Sir

Dublin (the Four Courts)

James Barrie, diminutive and melancholy, Kipling, nervous and ill-at-ease, Edmund Gosse, A. E. Housman, and Galsworthy. Dublin, where he was born, and St Pancras, where he lived until his forties, suddenly remembered their son and conferred their Freedoms on him.

There were beginning to be films of Shavian plays and broadcasts of them. In 1928 the Fox-Movietone film company made various attempts to persuade him to let himself be filmed. At last, having met with nothing but refusals, a team went down to Ayot St Lawrence and, with some difficulty, managed to gain entrance on the pretext of letting Shaw see their fascinating equipment.

Bust of Shaw by Jacob Epstein

Charlotte in old age

They could not have hit on a happier device; he was enchanted with the cameras and other instruments, as he always was with machinery, and eventually said that he would not so much mind being filmed, if only he might do it in his own way. The film-makers eagerly asked how he would set about it. He told them he would start by showing himself walking slowly up the garden towards the camera. . . . In the space of a few moments they had actually filmed his idea. From then until his ninetieth birthday he often appeared in short newsreel films and once in a trailer—the American trailer for his *Major Barbara*.

The broad stream of books on the subject of Shaw the playwright, the Socialist, the thinker, the idiot, and so forth, was beginning to pour out upon an eager market. Chesterton's had been published as early as 1909, Julius Bab's in 1926; Henderson's monument to thoroughness came in 1932, Walker's in 1933, Rattray's work in 1934, Frank Harris's in 1934, Caudwell's in 1938, Hesketh Pearson's in 1942, to name only a few—biography after biography, attack after attack, adulation after adulation, Marxist points of view, Christian points of view, personal points of view.

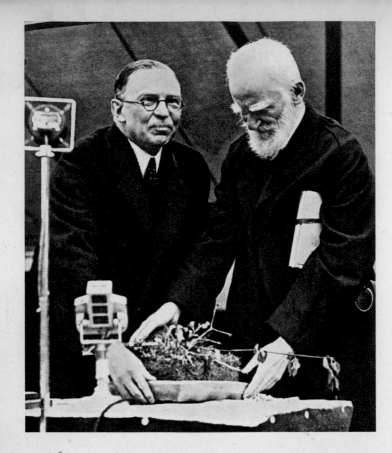

Very early in his career Shaw began to urge that there should be a National Theatre. Here Sir Robert Vansittart is handing the 'deeds' of the site for the proposed theatre to Shaw.
It has not yet been built.

Meanwhile, between unveiling memorials to Shakespeare and receiving the deeds of a site for the National Theatre (as yet still unbuilt), presiding over meetings, and attending dinners for the great, he returned once again to the old theme: Socialism.

In 1928, the year in which women finally got the vote on an equal footing with men, his sister-in-law, Mary Cholmondely, asked if he would write her a small pamphlet for a Women's Institute lecture on the subject. He began on it but soon realized that here was material for a book, if not a whole library. For three years he laboured on, and the final result was *The Intelligent Woman's Guide to Socialism and Capitalism*, a five-hundred-page summing-up of all the views on economic and political theory for which he and the Fabians had so long done battle. He found the writing a strain; he was now in his seventies and the patient amassing of fact after fact, the building-up of argument after argument tired him and caused Charlotte to wish devoutly that the book were finished. Eventually, writes his secretary, Blanche Patch, he wrote the words 'The End' and she asked him how he felt. He answered: 'I threw down my pen and said to Charlotte, "It's bloody well finished."'

'The Intelligent Woman's Guide'

Shaw and Lady Astor being entertained by a group of well-known Russian writers during their visit to the Soviet Union in 1931

He had an opportunity of seeing Socialism in practice when in 1931 he visited the Soviet Union with Lord and Lady Astor and their son. He was much impressed by what he saw (though he disliked the new cult accorded to Socialist deities such as Lenin) and scouted any suggestion that a special performance of prosperity had been laid on for him. In contrast to the English, the Russians received him as an old-fashioned bourgeois, but nevertheless treated him with politeness. In fact, more than four thousand people gathered in the Hall of Nobles to do him honour with a reception which he called 'a queer mixture of public meeting, snack bar, banquet and concert'. The climax of the visit was an audience with Stalin. *Soviet Union*

The sage of drama was no longer forced to hawk his plays about to London managements. He had a festival of his own—the Malvern Festival founded by Barry Jackson in 1927—for which he wrote *The Apple Cart*, a portrayal of *'The Apple Cart'*

The summer school of the Independent Labour Party: Shaw speaking on his visit to Russia

the oddities of 'democratic' government in practice, rather than in theory. The astuteness and superior reasoning powers of King Magnus led the super-ficially-minded to jump at the conclusion that Shaw was becoming a Royalist in his old age; he had not lost his talent for disconcerting those who thought they 'understood' and sympathized with him, as he had disconcerted the pro-Boers, the militant atheists, the anti-mysticism scientists. The play was a success, although the strain of production, in which he took as active a part as ever, told on him.

But it was Shaw's last great success in the theatre. The plays that followed it had something of the old man's garrulousness and repetitiveness which he saw and bemoaned in himself, even if his self-description as 'deaf and doddering and dotty' was an exaggeration.

Lawrence of Arabia   In *Too True to be Good*, first produced at the Malvern Festival in 1932, he used Lawrence of Arabia as a model for one of the characters, Private Meek.

T. E. Lawrence,
with whom the Shaws
became very friendly

They met first by chance, when Sir Sydney Cockerell, having to collect one of Augustus John's portraits of Shaw for the Fitzwilliam Museum and expecting Shaw himself to be out, took Lawrence round to the flat in Adelphi Terrace. Lawrence, the hero of the Arabian campaign, was now merely 'Aircraftman Shaw', having returned to the ranks after his terrible experiences in the Middle East. (Later Shaw inscribed a book to him 'To Private Shaw from Public Shaw.') Almost before the acquaintance had begun Lawrence sent Shaw the manuscript of his *Seven Pillars of Wisdom* for his opinion. Shaw was delighted with it and despite the pressure of his own work made several suggestions; but Charlotte was even more entranced and from that time onwards adopted Lawrence as a sort of honorary son. With great enthusiasm but some lack of

A stained-glass window (in the Ethical church)
incorporating portraits of St Joan and Shaw

insight, she suggested first that Barrie, and then that Shaw himself, might write a preface to *The Seven Pillars of Wisdom*. She and Lawrence corresponded regularly and she collected newspaper articles in which he was mentioned. She was also one of the few people to whom he showed the manuscript of *The Mint*. They discussed books and music; she sent him records to play in his R.A.F. camp and delicacies of various kinds to relieve the monotony of R.A.F. food. It was she and Shaw who gave him the motor-cycle on which he finally met his death.

Death was beginning to maroon Shaw on an island in the midst of an alien sea of juniors. Ellen Terry had died in 1928. His dearly-loved friend William Archer, his old fellow-campaigner for Ibsen, died in 1925, Hyndman, the middle-class Socialist, in 1921. His sister Lucy, the one member of the family who, in the early days, had seemed destined for a great career, died in 1920. There had been little contact between her and the Shaws for a long time: she and Charlotte did not care for each other and she had, besides, acquired a bitter cynicism in the course of her marital and professional failures which shocked even Shaw. But he was nevertheless moved by the manner of her death.

Shaw with Sidney and Beatrice Webb

'We were silent then; and there was no sound except from somebody playing the piano in the nearest house (it was a fine evening and all the windows were open) until there was a very faint flutter in her throat. She was still holding my hand. Then her thumb straightened. She was dead. . . . I asked [the doctor] what cause of death he would put in the certificate, adding that I supposed it was tuberculosis, from which she had suffered for many years following an attack of pneumonia which had ended her stage career. . . . He said "No . . . starvation."'

It emerged that she had been badly shell-shocked in the First World War and since that time had never eaten enough to keep herself alive. His father had been an alcoholic, his sister a pitiful and self-pitying failure; Shaw, on the other hand, stamped vigorously on, treading on corns if necessary but always bounding joyously back into action again.

Shaw's next work almost severed his friendship with the Abbess of Stanbrook, and alienated the affections of many others besides. It was *The Adventures of the Black Girl in her Search for God*, a fantasy on the subject of the

'Adventures of the Black Girl'

Shaw arriving in South Africa
where he wrote *The Adventures of the
Black Girl in her Search for God*

various gods set up by different parts of the Old and New Testaments. Its underlying spirituality was undeniable; the very fact that the quest for God was the central theme should have been enough to show Shaw's intense interest in the needs of the soul; but the lack of prejudice with which he approached the task antagonized professed believers of almost every sect. The Abbess could only ask wistfully for the withdrawal of the book and an act of public reparation which she knew she would not get.

The book was written as the result of an accident. The Shaws were visiting South Africa in 1932 when he, driving Mrs Shaw, pressed the accelerator instead of the footbrake, turned the steering-wheel the wrong way and landed the car and his wife in a predicament from which it took Charlotte some time to recover. As she lay recovering from a dent in the shin, bruises, sprains, two black eyes, and a temperature of 103 degrees, Shaw filled in the time by writing *The Adventures of the Black Girl*.

Shaw in Hollywood with (left to right) Charlie Chaplin, Marion Davies, Louis B. Mayer, Clark Gable, and George Hearst

Shaw entertained by the Governor of Manila   Shaw with Sir Ho Tung in Hong Kong

When his plays began to be filmed Shaw (eighty in this picture) took a great interest in the new medium. Here he is shown at a rehearsal for *Pygmalion*

His travels with Charlotte began, in his old age, to take up a good deal of his time. Together they visited India, New Zealand, Egypt, and America, where he offended many by not wishing to give the numerous speeches and lectures demanded of him, although he did in fact deliver his last oration there—'a quite successful ninety minutes spellbinding; but I was tired for three days after it and knew I was too old for the game'. At home his life was becoming more sober; a good many of his old friends were dead or inaccessible and his social activities, consequently, were limited. But he still retained the power of irritating the conventional almost beyond endurance. In 1936, for instance,

The Abdication George V died and Edward VIII occupied the throne for a brief period before being forced to quit it on his marriage to a divorced commoner, Mrs Simpson. Shaw's comment on the affair was contained in a short dialogue for the *Evening Standard* entitled 'The King, the Constitution and the Lady', in which he lightly blew away all obstacles to the union, including the impossibility of marriage in a church; his King welcomed a registry office ceremony because it would be so much more acceptable to the large proportion of his subjects who were not Christians. The descendants of the stalwart citizens who had made Irving into a religious institution and paid feudal homage to the figures of Mackenzie, Sullivan, and Parry, were more than outraged.

However, they took it as a matter of course that Shaw the playwright should be courted by the new medium which began in the year of Edward VIII's abdication. In 1937 Shaw supervised the rehearsals for the first television production of one of his plays, *How He Lied To Her Husband*.

Meanwhile the situation in Europe was worsening; yet another war with Germany was imminent. In 1938 Neville Chamberlain signed a pact with Hitler at Munich and in 1939 the Second World War began, despite Shaw's assurance, given in a letter to *The Times*, that the pact between Russia and Germany made it impossible. Children and schools were evacuated from the great cities into the country, bombs fell and destroyed, driving people into a greater camaraderie and friendliness than had been known before; austerity and rationing became the commonplaces of life. When almost the whole of Britain was engrossed and united by a single aim, broader questions, questions outside

World War II

Shaw on the set during the filming of *How He Lied To Her Husband*

Shaw with Charlie Chaplin at the première of *City Lights* at the Dominion Theatre, London

the immediate issue, lost in importance. Suddenly everything from 'Before-the-War' acquired a curious period flavour which, with the advent of the hydrogen bomb, the Cold War, and the greatly improved material conditions of the post-war years, it has kept. *Everybody's Political What's What*, published in 1944, reiterated a good many of the themes in *The Intelligent Woman's Guide* but in the circumstances it was little regarded.

His popularity during the war years was also diminished by the admiration he had paraded in recent plays and prefaces (such as *Geneva*) for the strength of dictators, in particular Mussolini. While he had been quick to denounce the more horrific aspects of their policies, he was still haunted by a feeling that a truly strong man could do what a multitude of committees and councils could not. But the public had no time to probe into the finesses of his arguments and motives; as usual in a time of real national crisis, it dismissed his views as irrelevant or even harmful.

Life at Ayot, where the Shaws stayed all the time during the war, continued fairly uneventfully. A few bombs hurtled into neighbouring fields and woods, a few suggestions were made that evacuees might be billeted on the Shaws, but

Shaw in old age

otherwise everything was much as usual. During the morning Shaw worked, often in his shelter in the garden; in the afternoon he rested; in the evening he and Charlotte listened to the wireless or went to the local cinema. His secretary, two maids, a housekeeper, and gardener completed the establishment.

By now his great age had aggravated some of the peculiarities that had always been part of his character. He had become terrified of financial ruin, practised small and useless economies and was convinced that he paid £147 income tax for every £100 he earned.

'Through the invention of the cinematograph [he wrote], I lately received a further windfall of £29,000 on account of my film rights. The financial result was that I had to pay £50,000 to the Chancellor of the Exchequer within two years. And the result of the catastrophe is that I am now using my copyrights ... to forbid and suppress them in order to reduce my income to a point at which it will be possible for me to live on it.'

Films

The film referred to was *Pygmalion*, the third play by Shaw to be filmed but the first overwhelming success. For a long time he had held out against the overtures of Hollywood, since each producer stipulated that he must be allowed to make whatever changes in the text he pleased. Eventually, however, he gave way, to a Hungarian producer, Gabriel Pascal, although he insisted on supervising every alteration made to the text, even at the age of eighty-two.

Shaw with Gabriel Pascal (who produced the film of *Pygmalion*), Leslie Howard, and Lady Oxford

Pygmalion was a huge success and when Shaw visited Pinewood studios, where it was made, he was fêted by a hundred guests, including Lady Oxford, Anthony Asquith and, of course, the stars of the film.

Death of Charlotte

In 1943 Charlotte died after a long and painful illness, osteitis deformans. This had followed almost immediately after Shaw himself had been severely ill with pernicious anaemia. To cure this he was given liver injections which caused him, as a conscientious vegetarian, much concern, although not nearly as much as the hundreds of vegetarians who had made him their prophet and standard-bearer. Despite the enforced injections, however, Shaw never fully regained his old strength and Charlotte's death weakened him still further. She was cremated at Golders Green.

It was a time of deaths and endings. In 1946 H. G. Wells died at the comparatively trivial age of sixty-eight. Chesterton had died as early as 1936. And in 1947 Sidney Webb (now Lord Passfield) also died, so that Shaw's closest old Fabian associates were now all gone.

Shaw working in
his summer-house at
the age of ninety

In 1949, after an illness which began when he broke his leg while pruning a
tree at Ayot St Lawrence, Shaw himself died. He was mourned and reminisced
about, regretted and patronized. The Indian Cabinet adjourned and the lights
of Broadway were put out for a few moments as a token of mourning. .

His posthumous career has followed a predictably unpredictable pattern.
For a while he was unfashionable in literary circles, particularly with the
movements which tended to make a virtue of their own inarticulateness; they
disliked him because his meaning, however unclear, is always clearly expressed.
A little later he became fashionable with another group as a 'period' playwright,
conjuring up visions, in the sentimental mind, of long-dead gracious living—
visions which provided suitable material for such immensely popular musicals
as *My Fair Lady*, for lavish films and television adaptations. In the meantime
there was much discussion about Shaw's will, with its bequest for the creation
of a new, phonetic alphabet. Did English require a phonetic alphabet? Does
one, in fact, recognize words by the individual letters or by the shape of the
word as a whole? Is increased speed of reading advisable? These were some of
the questions the bequest raised, and, like most of Shaw's questions, the answers
to them were less important than the fact that they were asked at all. A competition

Shaw's death

Shaw's Corner

was held to find the script Shaw wanted and this has now been devised. One might assume, therefore, that the problem is now solved, like so many other problems Shaw had dealt with at various times—slum-landlordship, for instance, or a musical scene dominated by drawing-room performances of 'The Lost Chord', or totally unreasonable stage-censorship.

However, the fact that many of Shaw's themes are of period interest only, does not mean that, as an artist, he can no longer be said to be of interest. The test is, surely, whether his plays, whatever their theme, still have the power to arouse amusement, sympathy, and interest, whether their action and dialogue still retain enough dramatic force and shock to keep an audience thoroughly interested and involved. Needless to say, not all of Shaw's many plays still have this power; but some—*Pygmalion*, *Man and Superman*, and *St Joan*, for instance—are still sufficiently forceful, sufficiently adroit in their use of comic shock and disclosure of true motives behind the mask put on for convention's sake, to make their point to this day. Shaw the sociologist, Shaw the politician, Shaw the crank—all these may blend into their period background and be forgotten, but some of his plays and some of his critical writings will continue to be of importance as long as the English-speaking nations have a taste for good writing.

1856 Birth of Shaw at 33 Synge Street, Dublin.

1868 The Shaw family shares a house with Vandaleur Lee at 1 Hatch Street, Dublin.

1871 Becomes a clerk in the estate agents' firm of Charles Uniacke Townshend.

1872 Mrs Shaw and her two daughters go to London and Shaw and his father move into lodgings at 61 Harcourt Street.

1875 Writes letter to the Press on the subject of Moody and Sankey.

1876 Joins his mother at 13 Victoria Grove, Fulham Road, London.

1879 Employed by Edison Telephone Company for a few months. Makes his first speech (at the Zetetical Society). Writes his first novel, *Immaturity*.

1880 Writes his second novel, *The Irrational Knot*.

1881 Becomes a vegetarian under Shelley's influence and writes his third and fourth novels, *Love Among the Artists* and *Cashel Byron's Profession*.

1883 Writes his fifth novel (incomplete), *An Unsocial Socialist*.

1884 Foundation of the Fabian Society, which he joins.

1885 He and his mother and sister move to 29 Fitzroy Square. His father dies. He becomes a member of the Executive Committee of the Fabian Society. Reviews books for the *Pall Mall Gazette*. Is seduced by Mrs Jenny Patterson and begins *Widowers' Houses*.

1886 Is art critic for the *World*.

1887 Edits the *Fabian Essays* (writing two of them), and writes *Don Giovanni Explains*.

1888 Is music critic for the *Star*, writing under the name of Corno di Bassetto.

1889 They move to 36 Osnaburgh Street. *Fabian Essays* published.

1890 Music critic for the *World* under his own name.

1891 Writes *The Quintessence of Ibsenism*.

1892 *Widowers' Houses* is given two performances by the Independent Theatre Society. He begins his correspondence with Ellen Terry.

1893 He writes *The Philanderer*, and *Mrs Warren's Profession*.

1894 Leaves the *World* and writes *Arms and the Man* and *Candida*. *Arms and the Man* performed for eleven weeks but makes a loss of over £2,000.

1895 Is dramatic critic on the *Saturday Review* and writes *The Man of Destiny*, *You Never Can Tell*, and *The Sanity of Art*. *Candida* is performed.

1896 He meets Charlotte Payne-Townshend and writes *The Devil's Disciple*.

1897 He becomes a vestryman of St Pancras and *The Man of Destiny* and *The Devil's Disciple* are performed in Croydon and New York respectively.

1898 Leaves the *Saturday Review*, marries Charlotte, writes *Caesar and Cleopatra* and publishes *Plays Pleasant and Unpleasant* and *The Perfect Wagnerite.*

1899 Writes *Captain Brassbound's Conversion. You Never Can Tell* is performed by the Stage Society.

1900 St Pancras is made a borough, *Fabianism and the Empire* published, and *Captain Brassbound's Conversion* performed.

1901 Writes *The Admirable Bashville* and begins *Man and Superman. Caesar and Cleopatra* is performed.

1903 Leaves the St Pancras Borough Council and finishes *Man and Superman.* H. G. Wells joins the Fabians.

1904 Writes *The Commonsense of Municipal Trading, John Bull's Other Island,* and *How He Lied To Her Husband.* Defeated as Progressive candidate for the L.C.C. Vedrenne and Barker take over the management of the Royal Court Theatre.

1905 Writes *Major Barbara* and moves into his house at Ayot St Lawrence.

1906 Writes *The Doctor's Dilemma* and sits to Rodin. Ellen Terry first appears in *Captain Brassbound.*

1907 Writes *Interlude at the Playhouse* and publishes *Aerial Football.*

1908 Writes *Getting Married.*

1909 Writes *The Shewing-Up of Blanco Posnet* and *Misalliance.* Member of the Parliamentary Committee on stage censorship.

1910 Writes *The Dark Lady of the Sonnets.*

1911 Writes *Fanny's First Play* and resigns from the Executive Committee of the Fabian Society.

1912 Writes *Androcles and the Lion, Overruled,* and *Pygmalion.* Proposes a pact between Britain, France, and America to settle all grievances.

1913 Death of his mother. Writes *Great Catherine* and begins *Heartbreak House.* The *New Statesman* is founded.

1914 Beginning of the First World War. *Commonsense About the War* makes him unpopular.

1916 Writes *O'Flaherty, V.C., The Inca of Perusalem,* and *Augustus Does His Bit.*

1917 Writes *Annajanska, the Bolshevik Empress.*

1918 End of War. Women of thirty and over given the vote. Begins *Back to Methuselah.*

1919 Finishes *Heartbreak House.*

1920 His sister Lucy dies. Finishes *Back to Methuselah.*

1922 Translates Trebitsch's *Frau Gittas Sühne.*

1923 Writes *St Joan,* performed in New York with great success.

1926 General Strike. He is awarded the Nobel Prize for literature.

1928 Publishes *The Intelligent Woman's Guide to Socialism.*

1929 Writes *The Apple Cart.* The first Malvern Festival takes place.

1931 Writes *Too True to be Good.* Visits Russia with the Marquess of Lothian and Viscount and Viscountess Astor.

1932 Visits South Africa and writes *The Adventures of the Black Girl in her Search for God.*

1933 Visits America and writes *On the Rocks* and *A Village Wooing*.

1934 Visits New Zealand and writes *The Six of Calais* and *The Simpleton of the Unexpected Isles*.

1935 Writes *The Millionairess*.

1936 Abdication of Edward VIII. Writes 'The King, the Constitution and the Lady' for the *Evening Standard*.

1938 Ill with pernicious anaemia. Writes *Geneva*.

1939 Writes *In Good King Charles' Golden Days*. Second World War begins: writes *Uncommonsense about the War*.

1943 Death of Charlotte. He writes *Everybody's Political What's What*.

1945 End of War.

1946 Begins *Buoyant Billions* and is made a Freeman of the Borough of St Pancras and the City of Dublin.

1947 Finishes *Buoyant Billions* and is elected to the Praesidium of the Prague Congress of the Union of Authors, Actors, and Journalists.

1949 Writes *Shakes versus Shav* and *Far-fetched Fables*.

1950 Begins *The Lady She Would Not*. Dies on 2nd November after a fall at his house at Ayot St Lawrence.

Frontispiece. After he had become famous Shaw sat to many painters, sculptors, and photographers. This portrait is by Augustus John. *Fitzwilliam Museum, Cambridge.*

Page

5   IT WAS IN KILLINEY BAY that Shaw's father gave him his first dip and one of his first lesson in *dégonflage*. 'When I was a boy of only fourteen my knowledge of swimming enabled me to save your Uncle Robert's life,' said Mr Shaw. And then, confidentially, 'And, to tell you the truth, I never was so sorry for anything in my life afterwards.' *By courtesy of the Irish Tourist Board.*

6   33 SYNGE STREET, DUBLIN. The plaque on the wall says 'Bernard Shaw, author of many plays, was born in this house 26 July 1856'.

7   GEORGE CARR SHAW, Shaw's father (extreme right), was born in 1814 and died in 1885. Although his continuous drinking caused the whole family much distress and his failure as a mill-owner reduced them to poverty and, to a certain extent, social isolation, Shaw nevertheless often referred to him with affection in his later writings, remembering his humour and lack of Victorian hypocrisy. Lucinda Elizabeth Shaw, Shaw's mother (extreme left), was born in 1830 and died in 1913. A talented amateur singer, she studied under George Vandaleur Lee in Dublin and when he moved to London followed him there in order to exploit her own and her daughter's musical talent. She eventually became music mistress at the North London Collegiate School. Shaw lived with her, and partly on her, until he married Charlotte Payne-Townshend in 1900. George Vandaleur Lee (seated, centre) differed from other singing-teachers of his day in not undertaking to turn every untutored miss into a Melba in the course of sixteen lessons. Superficial technical brilliance, unaccompanied by real musicality, did not interest him, any more than it did Shaw when he became a music critic. The atmosphere of music with which he, as an intimate of the family, surrounded the Shaws contributed much to Bernard's artistic awakening. After he moved to London in 1872 Lee lowered his standards but never achieved the success he had hoped for. *Radio Times Hulton Picture Library.*

8   SHAW (right) and Edward McNulty in 1874. They became friends when they were both thirteen and remained friendly all their lives. At one period McNulty even cherished a passion for Shaw's sister Lucy. *By courtesy of the University of North Carolina Library, U.S.A.*

9   THE VIEW OF DUBLIN BAY commanded by Torca Cottage gave Shaw enormous pleasure. It provided a striking contrast to the slum-like surroundings in which the Shaws lived in Dublin and was almost his first direct, profound experience of visual beauty. *By courtesy of the Irish Tourist Board.*

11   DWIGHT LYMAN MOODY and Ira David Sankey, the famous American evangelists, formed the subjects of Shaw's first published work—a letter to the Dublin *Public Opinion* on the occasion of their visit to the city in 1875. In this letter he challenged the efficacy of their methods. *Radio Times Hulton Picture Library.*

12   SHAW IN 1876 with John Gibbings, one of his fellow premium apprentices at Mr Uniacke Townshend's office. *By courtesy of Harold White.*

13   SHAW IN 1879—an excessively timid and awkward young man who was afraid to go into company and lived most of his life in

complete seclusion, attempting to write great novels and studying Wagner and Mozart. He was now living with his mother in London. *By courtesy of Harold White.*

14 THE JAEGER all-wool suit as ordered by Shaw on 17 June 1885. It was, he writes, 'the first new garment I have had for years', and he wore it in defiance of all the conventions which, at this period, demanded hot, tightly fitting clothes, with scratchy collars and constricting waistcoats. He maintained that his 'much ridiculed Jaegerism' was 'an attempt at cleanliness and porousness' and that 'cotton, linen and fibrous fabrics' collected odours. *By courtesy of The Jaeger Co. Ltd.*

15 WILLIAM ARCHER (1856–1924) was Ibsen's first English translator, a well-known critic, one of the first friends Shaw made in London, and the man who first suggested that Shaw write a play (in collaboration with himself). *Mander and Mitchenson Theatre Collection.*

16 KARL MARX (1818–83) was by no means the first to challenge accepted ideas of property and capitalism, but with his book *Das Kapital* (1867) he probably exerted a wider and more profound influence than any other thinker of his day. Although Shaw later rejected much of his economic theory, it was *Das Kapital* which effectively converted him to Socialism. *Radio Times Hulton Picture Library.*

17 HENRY MAYERS HYNDMAN was a philanthropist and the founder of one of the two other Socialist societies existing in London when the Fabian Society came into being. *Fabian Society Archives.*

18 SIDNEY WEBB was one of Shaw's earliest and closest friends, a Socialist and founder of the Fabian Society. He wrote copiously and minutely on economic matters. By profession he was a Civil Servant, eventually becoming Colonial Secretary and ending his life as a peer, Lord Passmore. BEATRICE WEBB, Sidney's wife, was an equally talented economist and sociologist. Born into a middle-class family, she had the courage to work for some time in an East End sweatshop to get first-hand experience of conditions; and her written work was as thorough as these practical experiences. *Radio Times Hulton Picture Library.*

19 THE WEBBS' HOUSE, 41 Grosvenor Road, was described (lightly disguised) by H. G. Wells in his novel *The New Machiavelli*, where he called it 'a hard little house'. In it the Webbs entertained most of the leading Fabians and Socialists, as well as eminent men from other political parties. It became, as it were, a deliberately inelegant and unfrivolous *salon*. *By courtesy of J. G. Miller.*

20 MRS ANNIE BESANT became a Fabian during the course of an extraordinary career beginning with highly emotional religiosity and ending with theosophy. To the late Victorians she was unmentionable for two reasons; her association with Charles Bradlaugh, the atheist, and her advocacy of birth control. Like many other women, she was bewitched by Shaw's attractions for a while. *Radio Times Hulton Picture Library.*

21 AS A RESULT of this Socialist demonstration in Dod Street, Limehouse, on Sunday 27 September 1885, Shaw was very nearly arrested. *Radio Times Hulton Picture Library.*

22 TITLE-PAGE of the Fabian Society's programme for 1886–7. *Fabian Society Archives.*

23 ON 'BLOODY SUNDAY', 13 November 1887, Shaw and other prominent Socialists led a march in protest against unemployment. They were beaten back by mounted police and generally roughly treated. This contemporary drawing shows the riot which developed. *Radio Times Hulton Picture Library.*

24 ONE OF SHAW'S CLOSEST FRIENDS, particularly before his marriage, was Henry Salt, who left Eton, where he was a housemaster, to devote himself to the simple life. He was a passionate vegetarian and animal-lover, a disciple of W. R. Hudson, Thoreau, and Shelley. Shaw was very fond of him and his wife Kate and frequently visited them at their primitive cottage at Tilford. This sketch of it is by Salt himself. *By courtesy of Hutchinson and Co. Ltd and S. Winsten.*

25 SHAW (seated) and Henry Salt. Salt, Kate, Shaw, Edward Carpenter, and Jim Joynes were united in their desire to overthrow traditional respectability and replace it by a simpler but more valid way of life. In 1888 Salt and Carpenter wrote a satirical 'Song of the Respectables' which was published in the *Pall Mall Gazette*. This photograph shows Shaw reading the song to Salt. *By courtesy of Hutchinson and Co. Ltd and S. Winsten.*

MRS JENNY PATTERSON, twelve years Shaw's senior, and one of his mother's pupils, relieved him of his virginity when he was twenty-nine and made a nuisance of herself long after he had ceased to feel anything for her. *London Express News and Feature Services.*

26 FLORENCE FARR was a well-known actress at the turn of the century. She played in more than one of Shaw's plays including *Arms and the Man*. At one period he fell in love with her. She is shown here as she appeared in *Sicilian Idyll* in 1891. *The Enthoven Collection. By courtesy of the Victoria and Albert Museum.*

27 E. (EDITH) NESBIT, like her husband, Hubert Bland, was an early member of the Fabian Society. She was also an inspired writer of children's books. She, too, fell under the spell of Shaw's charm for a short period. *By courtesy of Ernest Benn Ltd.*

28 THE HAMMERSMITH SOCIALIST LEAGUE with William Morris. Morris (the poet and designer) is fourth from the right in the second row from the front. *By courtesy of the Victoria and Albert Museum. Crown copyright reserved.*

29 MAY MORRIS was one of the very few women who bewitched Shaw instead of being bewitched by him. *By courtesy of the Victoria and Albert Museum. Crown copyright reserved.*

31 ADELINA PATTI, one of the virtuosi who dominated the musical scene in London at the end of the last century when Shaw was working as a music critic. He put up a strong fight for more musicality and musicianship in performance, and, of course, championed Wagner. *Radio Times Hulton Picture Library.*

32 SHAW in the 1880's. *Radio Times Hulton Picture Library.*

33 SARAH BERNHARDT (1825–1923) was one of the most famous actresses of her day but Shaw criticized her severely for the way she usually sacrificed the play to her own virtuoso effects, and preferred stupid display pieces to worth-while drama. This picture shows her as Pelléas in Maeterlinck's *Pelléas et Mélisande*.

34 THIS CONTEMPORARY DRAWING shows how, at the end of the nineteenth century, the theatre was chiefly a place for the display of a fashionable toilette and the exchange of fashionable scandal. Shaw spoke out boldly against this attitude in his criticisms for the *Saturday Review. Radio Times Hulton Picture Library.*

35 HENRIK IBSEN (1828–1906) was the favourite *avant-garde* playwright of the nineties. Shaw admired him intensely because he had reintroduced an element of serious purpose into drama which for most of the nineteenth century had been condemned to insipid frivolity: *The Quintessence of Ibsenism* was written in 1891. Although at first Ibsen's plays (like Shaw's) were denounced as filth by conventional critics they eventually exerted

a profound influence on British drama. *Radio Times Hulton Picture Library.*

36 THE ORIGINAL theatre programme for Shaw's *Widowers' Houses,* first performed in 1892. *The Enthoven Collection. By courtesy of the Victoria and Albert Museum.*

37 JACOB THOMAS GREIN (1863–1935) was a Jewish merchant of Dutch origin who founded the Independent Theatre Society with the avowed object of staging 'advanced' drama. His first performance was Ibsen's *Ghosts* and some time later the Society gave two performances of Shaw's *Widowers' Houses. Mander and Mitchenson Theatre Collection.*

38 IN THE EARLY YEARS of his career Shaw did much of his writing on trains and open-top buses like those shown here. *Radio Times Hulton Picture Library.*

39 AUBREY BEARDSLEY designed this programme for the Avenue Theatre season during which Shaw's *Arms and the Man* was first staged. It was his first play to be professionally performed in London. *Mander and Mitchenson Theatre Collection.*

ALMA MURRAY as Raïna in the first production of *Arms and the Man* (1894). *Mander and Mitchenson Theatre Collection.*

41 SHAW in the 1890's when, through his criticisms, he was becoming a man to be feared and respected by the theatrical world. *Elliott and Fry Ltd.*

42 EDWARD CARPENTER, 'the Noble Savage', was a close friend of the Salts, the Webbs, and Shaw. *By courtesy of Hutchinson and Co. Ltd and S. Winsten.*

43 GEORGE ALEXANDER, the very popular actor, was among the many people who

pronounced Shaw's *Candida* unactable. *Thames and Hudson Archives.*

45 ELLEN TERRY (shown here in 1897) was an outstanding actress and a woman of great charm. Shaw thought that she was wasted in Irving's productions of cut-about Shakespeare and jejune 'acting' plays and tried almost throughout his long and charming correspondence with her to get her to act in his own plays. In the end she played in *Captain Brassbound's Conversion,* which he had written for and around her. *Radio Times Hulton Picture Library.*

46 HENRY IRVING was, from quite early in his life, the Grand Old Man of the British Theatre. He was the first actor to be knighted (in 1895) and his performances of Shakespeare at the Lyceum came to be virtually uncriticizable, like Shakespeare himself. Nevertheless Shaw criticized them severely and reproached him with sacrificing Ellen Terry's talent as well as his own. Despite long negotiations, he never acted in *The Man of Destiny,* which Shaw wrote for him and Ellen, or any other of Shaw's plays. This cartoon by Max Beerbohm of Irving as a 'man of distinction' indicates his position in society at the turn of the century. *Ashmolean Museum, Oxford.*

47 ARTHUR CONAN DOYLE (whose Sherlock Holmes stories were already best-sellers) was happy to accept from Irving terms which Shaw (virtually unknown) treated with impudent scorn. *Radio Times Hulton Picture Library.*

48 HENRY IRVING as Richard III. Shaw's criticism of his performance in this role was taken by Irving's acolytes to mean that he was accusing Irving of drunkenness. Shaw's subsequent explanation did not undo the mischief altogether. *Radio Times Hulton Picture Library.*

49 MARGARET HALSTON as the Strange Lady in the first production of *The Man of Destiny*, the play Shaw wrote for Ellen Terry and Henry Irving, but which was never acted by them. *Mander and Mitchenson Theatre Collection.*

50 ELLEN TERRY as Lady Cicely Wayneflete in *Captain Brassbound's Conversion. Mander and Mitchenson Theatre Collection.*

51 H. G. WELLS in the 1890's when Shaw first met him. He joined the Fabian Society in 1903 and, in the opinion of the older-established members, proceeded to make a nuisance of himself. Unlike Shaw, he had first-hand experience of the trivial life of the lower middle classes, being the son of a housekeeper and unsuccessful shopkeeper, and he put this to good use in his best novels, *Love and Mr Lewisham*, *Kipps*, and *The History of Mr Polly*. He was also deeply interested in science, being virtually the first English science-fiction writer. In the early part of the century he, with Shaw and Chesterton, made up the supreme triumvirate of English letters. *Radio Times Hulton Picture Library.*

52 THE ST PANCRAS TOWN COUNCIL in session in 1900. Shaw was a zealous member of the Council for many years. He is shown here at the front of the right-hand table. *By courtesy of St Pancras Public Libraries.*

53 RICHARD MANSFIELD, a highly popular American actor-manager, as Dick Dudgeon in *The Devil's Disciple*. Mansfield gave the first American performance of several Shavian plays. *Mander and Mitchenson Theatre Collection.*

55 A SCENE FROM THE LAST ACT of *The Devil's Disciple* in the production at the Savoy Theatre in 1907. *Mander and Mitchenson Theatre Collection.*

56 ADELPHI TERRACE, where Charlotte Payne-Townshend had a flat (in No. 10). *By courtesy of the National Buildings Record.*

57 IN 1898 SHAW MARRIED Charlotte Payne-Townshend, a 'green-eyed Irish millionairess', and escaped from the uncomfortable squalor of Fitzroy Square to Adelphi Terrace where, according to Shaw, Charlotte had 'delightful rooms overlooking the river, over the London School of Economics'. By 1905, when this photograph was taken, Shaw had bought his home at Ayot St Lawrence. *Radio Times Hulton Picture Library.*

58 SHAW IN ABOUT 1901, the beginning of the era of prosperity. *Radio Times Hulton Picture Library.*

59 MR (LATER SIR) JOHNSTON FORBES-ROBERTSON as Caesar in Shaw's *Caesar and Cleopatra*. At first he expressed dislike of the play but he gave it its first professional production at the New Amsterdam Theatre, New York, in 1906. *Mander and Mitchenson Theatre Collection.*

60 THE RELIEF OF LADYSMITH celebrations. The Boer War aroused tremendous popular excitement and split the Fabian Society into at least two parties. As usual, Shaw's reaction was not what had been expected. *Radio Times Hulton Picture Library.*

61 SHAW'S CORNER at Ayot St Lawrence, Hertfordshire. This became the Shaws' country home in 1905 and towards the end of their lives they lived in it all the time. Its solid, square comfort contrasted sharply with the ill-organized squalor of Shaw's living quarters before he married Charlotte. *Keystone Press.*

62 THE HOUSE IN FITZROY SQUARE, where Shaw lived with his mother from 1887 until his marriage. The *ménage* was not a particularly happy one; its members held little communication with each other, and Shaw's room was, on the whole, left untouched and uncleaned. 'Whilst I am dressing and undressing I do all my reading. The book lies

open on the table. I never shut it, but put the next book on top of it long before its finished. After some months there is a mountain of buried books, all wide open, so that all my library is distinguished by a page with the stain of a quarter's dust or soot on it.' *By courtesy of St Pancras Public Libraries.*

63 SHAW IN HIS SUMMER-HOUSE at Ayot St Lawrence. One of Shaw's main complaints about the age in which he grew up was its physical stuffiness: the heavy, stifling clothes, the tightly shut windows, unhealthy diet, insanitarily fussy furniture, and general closed-in feeling. He himself flouted these conventions from the start and, on settling at Ayot, acquired the habit of working out-doors in this summer-house. *London News Agency.*

64 JOHN VEDRENNE managed the financial side of the Royal Court Theatre partnership and prudently restrained Granville-Barker's ex-travagance. *Mander and Mitchenson Theatre Collection.*

65 HARLEY GRANVILLE-BARKER was the pro-ducer of the plays put on at the Royal Court Theatre under his and John Vedrenne's management. He also acted in several of them, including many of Shaw's plays, wrote plays of his own and, in later life, the *Prefaces to Shakespeare*. He was one of the first producers to break away from the fussier stage traditions of the nineteenth century and stage Shakespeare's works practically uncut. In general his talent as a producer added greatly to the success of the plays put on at the Royal Court. *Radio Times Hulton Picture Library.*

66 WILLIAM BUTLER YEATS, at whose request Shaw wrote *John Bull's Other Island*, 'as a patriotic contribution to the repertory of the Irish Literary Theatre'. The tone of the play had nothing to do with the pseudo-Celtic

feeling aimed at by Yeats and his movement. In any case it was beyond the resources of the Abbey Theatre; it was first produced at the Royal Court on 1 November 1904. *Radio Times Hulton Picture Library.*

67 IT WAS THIS sort of open-air Salvation Army meeting, its martial music (though not the exhibitionism of the 'sinners') which Shaw found a more inspiring presentation of reli-gion than many cold and dusty church ser-vices. It provided him with one of the themes for *Major Barbara*. *By courtesy of the Salvation Army.*

68 SCENE FROM THE FIRST PRODUCTION (1906) of *The Doctor's Dilemma* at the Royal Court Theatre. *Mander and Mitchenson Theatre Collection.*

69 SCENE FROM THE 1906 REVIVAL of *How He Lied To Her Husband*, with Arnold Daly and Isabelle Urquhart. *Mander and Mitchenson Theatre Collection.*

70 ALFRED SUTRO and SIR ARTHUR WING PINERO were two of the dramatists with whom Shaw came into contact at the Dramatists' Club. He had criticized both strongly when he was working for the *Saturday Review* and they both, like the older generation in general, retained a certain feel-ing of antagonism towards him because of his rejection of all convention: he did so many things that were 'not done'. *Radio Times Hulton Picture Library.*

71 STILL FROM THE FILM *Masks and Faces* show-ing a meeting of the Council of the Royal Academy of Dramatic Art with, from left to right, Sir George Alexander, Barrie, Pinero, Irene Vanbrugh, Sir Squire Bancroft, C. M. Lawre (administrator of the Royal Academy), Shaw, Sir John Hare, and Sir Johnston Forbes-Robertson. *Mander and Mitchenson Theatre Collection.*

72 SHAW in his fifties. *Radio Times Hulton Picture Library.*

MARK TWAIN (Samuel L. Clemens) met Shaw by chance when he arrived at St Pancras Station. The reporter who was there to interview Twain lost no time in making their encounter into yet another newsworthy paragraph on Shaw. *Radio Times Hulton Picture Library.*

73 APART FROM their close artistic association with Shaw, Granville-Barker and his wife Lillah McCarthy were close personal friends of Shaw and Charlotte. This picture of Granville-Barker and Charlotte dates from 1909. *Mander and Mitchenson Theatre Collection.*

74 SHAW'S NAME or face was always appearing in the newspapers—either in a news item, or in a photograph, or, as here, in a cartoon (by Ruth). *Mander and Mitchenson Theatre Collection.*

75 SHAW WAS FASCINATED by mechanical gadgets of every kind. Indeed he once nearly bought a calculating machine for which he had no possible use, merely because the idea intrigued him. Like John Tanner in *Man and Superman*, he was very interested in cars, although he was not a particularly good driver. It was after involving himself and his wife in a fairly severe motor accident in South Africa that he wrote *The Adventures of the Black Girl in her Search for God*, while he was waiting for Charlotte to recover from her injuries. *London News Agency.*

76 HERBERT (NOW LORD) SAMUEL was Chairman of the Joint Select Committee of the House of Lords and the House of Commons on Stage Plays (Censorship) appointed in 1929 by the Liberal government. Shaw was one of the many eminent writers who contributed to the resultant Blue Book. *Radio Times Hulton Picture Library.*

77 SIR JAMES BARRIE lived opposite the Shaws, in London, although he did not often come into contact with them. However, he did persuade Shaw to take part in a burlesque of a Western film for the benefit of the Red Cross and Shaw's *Androcles and the Lion* was intended to rival Barrie's *Peter Pan* as an entertainment for children. *Radio Times Hulton Picture Library.*

78 KEIR HARDIE, the first Labour Member to be elected to Parliament (in 1892) with Mrs Shaw and Shaw. *By courtesy of Harold White.*

79 STATUE OF JOAN OF ARC at Orleans. During a visit to France in 1911 Shaw was deeply impressed by Orleans and the all-pervading memory of St Joan. He even toyed with the idea of writing a 'Joan play'; in fact *St Joan* was not written until some twenty years later. *French Government Tourist Office.*

81 MRS PATRICK CAMPBELL as Mrs Ebbsmith in *The Notorious Mrs Ebbsmith*. *The Enthoven Collection. By courtesy of the Victoria and Albert Museum.*

82 HERBERT BEERBOHM TREE, who created the role of Professor Higgins in *Pygmalion*, was an irritating man to work with in the Theatre. Despite various coolnesses, however, he and Shaw managed to create a production which was more successful than any previous Shaw plays. *The Enthoven Collection. By courtesy of the Victoria and Albert Museum.*

A PORTRAIT OF SHAW at the window of his study at Ayot St Lawrence. His great interest in the work of William Morris can be seen from the textiles; the window seat is upholstered in a 'Honeysuckle' fabric (designed 1876) while the curtains are the 'Compton' chintz, the last to be designed by Morris, in 1896.

83 MRS PATRICK CAMPBELL as Eliza Doolittle in *Pygmalion*, the play that Shaw wrote round

an idea suggested to him by a performance of hers given fifteen years before. *Mander and Mitchenson Theatre Collection.*

84 THE TITANIC being towed out on her trials. The sinking of the ship on her maiden voyage in 1912 and the loss of 1,490 lives incited Shaw to publish a 'rational' confutation of those who praised the heroism of the passengers and crew. Those whose reactions had been more emotional resented this bitterly. *Radio Times Hulton Picture Library.*

85 A CARTOON by Will Dyson depicting a Fabian debate between Shaw and Belloc. The second figure from the left is Hubert Bland, the fourth G. K. Chesterton, and the seventh Sidney Webb. *By courtesy of the Fabian Society.*

86 STILL FROM THE BURLESQUE of a Western in which Barrie persuaded Shaw to take part. It was made for the benefit of the Red Cross. From left to right: Lord Howard de Walden, William Archer, Barrie, Chesterton, and Shaw. *By courtesy of Harold White.*

87 CHARLOTTE in the first year of her marriage. This photograph was taken by Shaw himself. *By courtesy of Harold White.*

88 SHAW SWIMMING in the South of France while on holiday: one of the many Press photographs taken of him in every posture and circumstance after he had become 'news'. *Keystone Press.*

89 SHAW and GENE TUNNEY, the American heavyweight boxer, on holiday together. Although he thought most organized sport was puerile, Shaw had a great admiration for physical efficiency and power and himself continued to take a good deal of exercise until he was very old. He was friendly with Tunney for many years. *By courtesy of Harold White.*

90 SHAW IN THE PARTHENON with a group of Greek newspapermen who had come to interview him. Greece was among the many countries which Charlotte persuaded him to visit; he found little intrinsic interest in these travels. *By courtesy of Harold White.*

91 ANATOLE FRANCE and Shaw met accidentally in the Sistine Chapel. Shaw managed to disconcert France the man, as his works tended to disconcert France the nation. *Radio Times Hulton Picture Library.*

AUGUST STRINDBERG entertained Shaw in Stockholm but the two playwrights were so different in temperament that they found very little common ground. *Radio Times Hulton Picture Library.*

92 MRS PATRICK CAMPBELL (shown here with George Alexander in Pinero's *The Second Mrs Tanqueray*) almost succeeded in involving Shaw in an affair in 1912 and the following period; Sidney Webb called his infatuation with her 'a clear case of sexual senility'. Nevertheless Shaw returned to Charlotte before any lasting damage was done (to himself at least). *Thames and Hudson Archives.*

93 SHAW leaving His Majesty's Theatre after the production of his play *Pygmalion*. *P. A. Reuter.*

94 MRS PATRICK CAMPBELL in bed in her house in Kensington Square. This photograph was taken by Shaw himself. *By courtesy of Harold White.*

95 MRS PATRICK CAMPBELL's house in Kensington Square which Shaw haunted during his period of infatuation with its occupant. *By courtesy of the National Buildings Record.*

96 SCENE FROM the first production of *John Bull's Other Island*. Granville-Barker is second from the left. *Mander and Mitchenson Theatre Collection.*

97 A LATE PHOTOGRAPH (taken by Shaw himself) of his mother, who died in 1913. *By courtesy of Harold White.*

98 CROWDS CHEERING on the occasion of the declaration of war in 1914. The First World War sparked off many such demonstrations of patriotism. Shaw was one of the few to protest against the futility and mismanagement of the whole affair, and he became accordingly vastly unpopular with most people. *Radio Times Hulton Picture Library.*

99 THE FLANDERS FRONT in the 1914–18 War. Shaw visited the front at Field-Marshal Haig's invitation and was received more tolerantly by the men actually fighting than he had been by the public at home. *Radio Times Hulton Picture Library.*

100 JOSEPH CONRAD and ARNOLD BENNETT were among those of Shaw's personal friends who attacked him bitterly for his attitude towards the War and his remarks on the sinking of the *Lusitania. Radio Times Hulton Picture Library.*

101 SYLVIA PANKHURST addressing a crowd that had gathered round the Suffragettes' premises. In 1918 women of thirty got the vote. The Shaws had always been very sympathetic to the Suffragette cause, and Shaw had lectured on its behalf. *Radio Times Hulton Picture Library.*

102 ONE OF THE SUFFRAGETTE demonstrations (24 April 1913). *Radio Times Hulton Picture Library.*

103 SCENE FROM the first London production of *Heartbreak House* (1921). Edith Evans played Lady Utterword and is the fourth from the right in this picture. *Mander and Mitchenson Theatre Collection.*

104 SCENE FROM the first production of *Back to Methuselah* (by the Theatre Guild of New York in 1922). *Photo Vandamm.*

105 SIR SYDNEY COCKERELL, a friend of Shaw's, through whom he came to meet both the Abbess of Stanbrook and, later, T. E. Lawrence. *Elliott and Fry Ltd.*

106 THE ABBESS OF STANBROOK, Dame Laurentia MacLachlan, was an outstanding woman, with whom Shaw delighted to discuss questions of all kinds, since he greatly admired her wisdom and generosity of heart. *By courtesy of the Lady Abbess of Stanbrook Abbey and John Murray Ltd.*

107 STANBROOK ABBEY, to which Shaw went several times in order to talk with his friend the Abbess. *Photograph by Edward Ihnatowicz. By courtesy of the Lady Abbess of Stanbrook Abbey and John Murray Ltd.*

108 SYBIL THORNDIKE as St Joan in the first production of the play (1924). *Mander and Mitchenson Theatre Collection.*

109 WINIFRED LEUCHAN as St Joan in the New York Theatre Guild Production. *Mander and Mitchenson Theatre Collection.*

110 G. K. CHESTERTON and HILAIRE BELLOC were both distinguished writers and friends of Shaw. They shared a sufficient number of views for Shaw to nickname them 'the Chesterbelloc'. Public debates between Shaw, Chesterton, and Belloc were highly popular; on this occasion the subject of their debate was 'Do we agree?' *P.A. Reuter.*

111 NUMEROUS HONOURS were conferred on Shaw after he had become the British national sage. He was, for instance, made a Freeman of London, St Pancras, and Dublin (this picture shows the Four Courts, Dublin). *Radio Times Hulton Picture Library.*

112 SHAW was also portrayed in every possible medium—paintings, drawings, photographs, and sculptures were made of him. This bust is by Epstein. *Collection: Mr and Mrs Leo Schacter, Toronto. Photo: Hans Wild.*

113 A PHOTOGRAPH of Charlotte in old age taken by Shaw himself. *By courtesy of Harold White.*

114 SIR ROBERT VANSITTART handing the 'deeds' of the site of the proposed National Theatre to Shaw, in 1938. The 'deeds' were presented in the form of a sod and bunches of twigs—a revival of the custom of the Elizabethan period when formal deeds were unknown. The project for a National Theatre never came to anything and at last, in 1961, was formally abandoned by the government. *Central Press Photos Ltd.*

115 SHAW and LORD and LADY ASTOR visited the Soviet Union in 1931 and were given an enthusiastic reception in the Hall of Nobles and received by Stalin. Shaw and Lady Astor were also entertained by several notable Russian writers with whom they are shown here. *Photo by courtesy of the University of South Carolina.*

116 AFTER HIS VISIT to Russia, Shaw gave a talk on it at the summer school of the Independent Labour Party. This was held at Welwyn in September 1931. *P.A. Reuter.*

117 T. E. LAWRENCE met Shaw by chance, after his return to England. They became close friends. Shaw gave his opinion (a high one) on the writings which Lawrence was preparing for publication; and Mrs Shaw regarded him almost as an adopted son. Shaw based the character of Private Meek in *Too True to be Good* on him. *Central Press Photos Ltd.*

118 A STAINED-GLASS window in the Ethical Church, London. St Joan is the main subject and Shaw appears in the bottom left-hand portion. *P.A. Reuter.*

119 SHAW with Sidney Webb (then Lord Passfield) and Beatrice Webb in the 1930's. *Daily Herald.*

120 SHAW arriving in South Africa (1932), where he wrecked his car and, while waiting for Charlotte to recover from her injuries, wrote *The Adventures of the Black Girl in her Search for God.* Photo by courtesy of the University of North Carolina Library.

121 SHAW IN HOLLYWOOD, lunching with (from left to right) Charlie Chaplin, Marion Davies, Louis B. Mayer, Clark Gable, and George Hearst. *Keystone Press.*

WHEN HE WAS IN MANILA, during one of his many travels, Shaw was entertained by Theodore Roosevelt Jr., who was then Governor. *Fox Photos.*

SHAW with Sir Ho Tung in Hong Kong (1933). *P.A. Reuter.*

122 EVEN AT HIS ADVANCED AGE (eighty in this picture), Shaw continued to take an active interest in the filming of his plays. In this picture he is shown at a rehearsal for the film of *Pygmalion*, probably the most successful film made of one of his plays. Eliza Doolittle was played by Wendy Hiller, who is fourth from the right. *Mander and Mitchenson Theatre Collection.*

123 SHAW on the set at Elstree during the making of his *How He Lied To Her Husband*, the first of his plays to be filmed. *Mirrorpic.*

124 SHAW with Charlie Chaplin and Lady Astor at the première of *City Lights* made by Chaplin. *Mirrorpic.*

125 SHAW in old age. *Fox Photos Ltd.*

126 AT A LUNCHEON to inaugurate the filming of *Pygmalion*: Gabriel Pascal, the first film producer who succeeded in persuading Shaw that certain adjustments would have to be made to his plays if they were to be as artistically successful on the screen as on the stage; Shaw, Leslie Howard (who played

Professor Higgins), and Lady Oxford. *Keystone Press.*

127 SHAW in 1946, when he was ninety, working in his summer-house at Ayot St Lawrence. *Central Press Photos.*

128 SHAW'S CORNER at Ayot St Lawrence, where his ashes and those of his wife lie scattered. He bequeathed the house to the National Trust in his will. *Keystone Press.*